A HISTORY LOVER'S GUIDE TO NORTH CAROLINA

MICHAEL C. HARDY

Published by The History Press
Charleston, SC
www.historypress.com

First published 2022

Manufactured in the United States

ISBN 9781467151641

Library of Congress Control Number: 2022933372

Notice: The information in this book is true and complete to the best of our knowledge. It is offered without guarantee on the part of the author or The History Press. The author and The History Press disclaim all liability in connection with the use of this book.

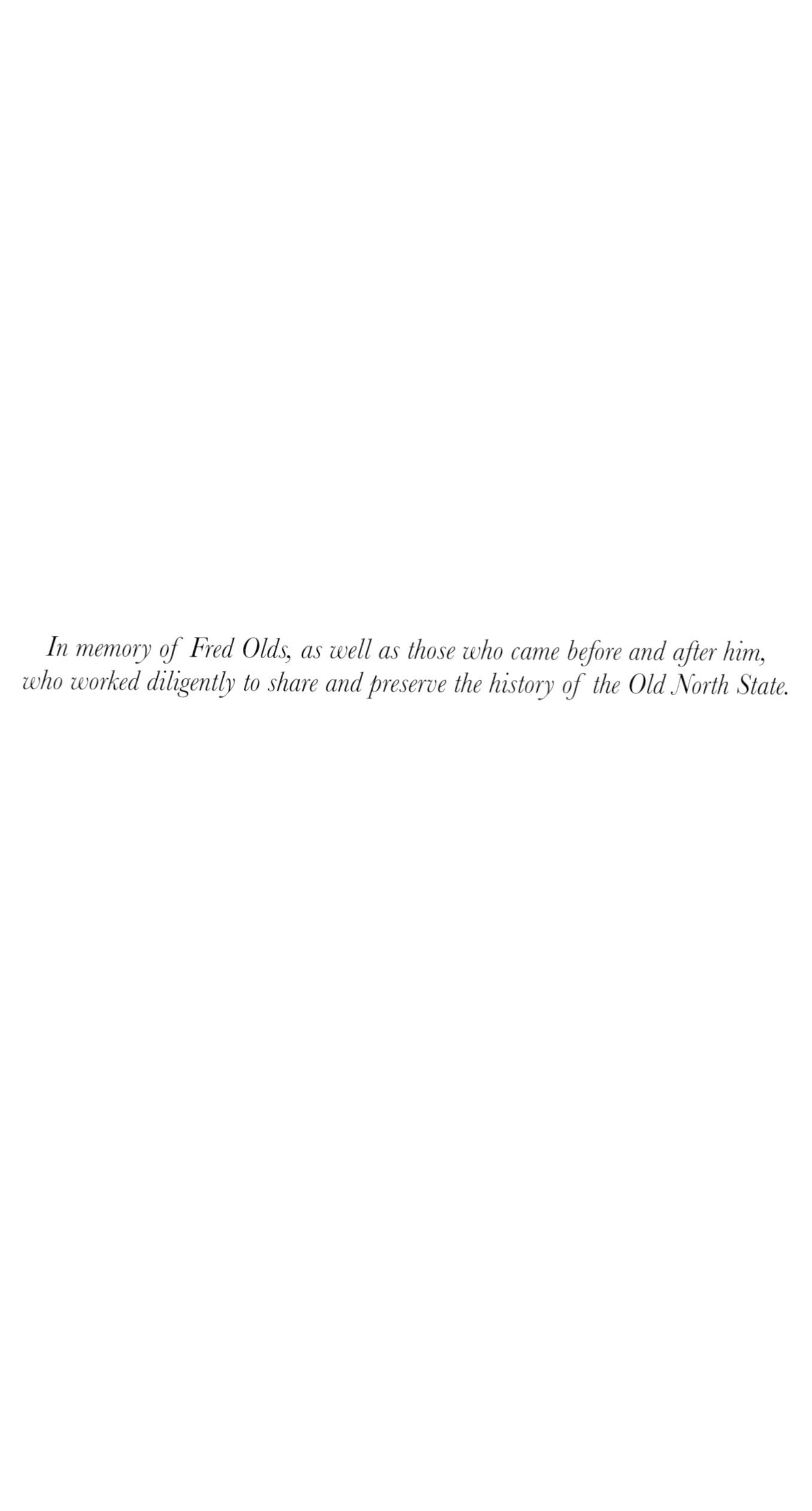

In memory of Fred Olds, as well as those who came before and after him,
who worked diligently to share and preserve the history of the Old North State.

CONTENTS

INTRODUCTION

We all owe a great deal of gratitude to Frederick Olds (1853–1935). Olds grew up in Hillsborough, North Carolina; attended the Virginia Military Institute; worked as a reporter and editor of the Raleigh *News and Observer*; and served on the staff of Governor Zebulon Baird Vance. Captivated by history, he began collecting land grants, court records and portraits in the 1880s, depositing the items in the state library. By 1930, the collection numbered thirty thousand items. Olds is considered the "Father of the North Carolina Museum of History." The museum was simply called the Hall of History in his time. But Olds did more than collect artifacts. He traveled across the state, talking to local people and writing the histories of the areas he visited. Of course, there were other historians before Olds, and many have come after, but so much of what we have and know today is a product of Olds's interest.

What Olds revealed was that North Carolina is an amazing place. From the highest peak east of the Mississippi River to the largest sounds along the Eastern Seaboard, from pirates and presidents to astronauts and civil rights leaders, the natural and human history of the Old North State is vast. It is also easy to explore. There are more than five hundred historic sites and museums and more than one thousand historic markers and monuments across the Tar Heel State. This book does not begin to cover them all and does not go into minute detail about the sites included, but it is my hope that this volume will create a spark for those interested to get out and explore the rich history of North Carolina.

This book focuses primarily on people and places of the past, a past that is sometimes troublesome and always complicated. While some popular subjects—like musician Randy Travis, actress Ariana DeBose and author Nicholas Sparks—could have been included, they are still living and writing their own stories. Hence, for most categories, only individuals who are deceased are included. Some of the topics mentioned are the themes of entire museums and historic sites, while others are the subjects of highway historical markers.

In the midst of the COVID-19 pandemic in 2021, itself a part of history, this project was born. This timing presented certain challenges. Museums and historic sites have been closed, opened, opened with restrictions and, in a few cases, permanently closed. However, my research for this book actually started decades ago. In 1995, we moved to Boone and, in 2001, to Avery County. We began to explore and volunteer at historic sites across the state. It was at the same time that I began to write about North Carolina. Our sense of community service, coupled with the research needed to write more than two dozen books, took us to many places, from Fort Fisher to the Zebulon Baird Vance Birthplace near Weaverville. My interest is more than just that of a researcher, writer, interpreter and visitor. Parts of my family were living in the Surry and Wilkes Counties area in the 1760s and 1770s. Some of them marched with Colonel Benjamin Cleveland to join the Overmountain Men and fight in the Battle of Kings Mountain. So, in some small way, parts of this story are my story as well.

Visiting historic sites is a wonderful experience, and it is even better when one is a little prepared and can avoid possible disappointments. A visitor hoping to visit any historical site or museum should either check the organization's website or call before visiting, as hours fluctuate, and questions about admission, parking and accessibility can be resolved in advance.

Many of the chapters in this tome are divided up into three sections based on geography. The counties included in the coastal region are Beaufort, Bertie, Bladen, Brunswick, Camden, Carteret, Chowan, Columbus, Craven, Currituck, Dare, Duplin, Gates, Greene, Hertford, Hyde, Jones, Lenoir, Martin, New Hanover, Onslow, Pamlico, Pasquotank, Pender, Perquimans, Pitt, Tyrrell and Washington. The Piedmont counties include Alamance, Alexander, Anson, Cabarrus, Caswell, Catawba, Chatham, Cumberland, Davidson, Davie, Durham, Edgecombe, Forsyth, Franklin, Gaston, Granville, Guilford, Halifax, Harnett, Hoke, Iredell, Johnston, Lee, Lincoln, Mecklenburg, Montgomery, Moore, Nash, Northampton, Orange, Person, Randolph, Richmond, Robeson, Rockingham, Rowan, Sampson,

Scotland, Stanly, Stokes, Surry, Union, Vance, Wake, Warren, Wayne, Wilson and Yadkin. Mountain and foothill counties include Alleghany, Ashe, Avery, Buncombe, Burke, Caldwell, Cherokee, Clay, Cleveland, Graham, Haywood, Henderson, Jackson, Macon, Madison, McDowell, Mitchell, Polk, Rutherford, Swain, Transylvania, Watauga, Wilkes and Yancey.

A special thanks to all of the librarians who have kept the state's history and made it accessible, and also to those who oversee the hundreds of historic sites and museums across North Carolina, presenting the state's history in a tangible way. Thanks also to my readers: Travis Souther and, as always, Elizabeth Baird Hardy.

FROM THE MOUNTAINS TO THE SEA

THE GEOGRAPHY OF NORTH CAROLINA

North Carolina can be divided up into several different geographic regions: Tidewater, Inner Coastal Plain, Sandhills, Piedmont, Foothills and Mountains. Every region is rich in diversity with plenty of places to explore, only a few of which are listed here. The North Carolina Museum of Natural Sciences in Raleigh is a great place to discover the different topographies and ecosystems throughout North Carolina. Originally opened in 1879, the museum contains more than 1.7 million specimens and exhibits on prehistoric North Carolina, an arthropod zoo, a theater and information on the tools and techniques used by naturalists over the past one hundred years. Many of the displays and labs offer hands-on experiences.

COASTAL

There are roughly 322 miles of coastline along the eastern edge of North Carolina. Much of this area is famously known as the Outer Banks, a chain of barrier islands that are as much as 30 miles from the mainland and separated by a series of shallow sounds. The islands are constantly changing, largely due to the storms that open and close inlets. Native Americans sparsely inhabited the far reaches of the Outer Banks but lived in larger numbers along the inner coastal areas.

Carolina Beach State Park, New Hanover County

Prior to the arrival of Europeans, Cape Fear Indians inhabited the area. In 1715, the natives rose against settlers in the area, a war they lost. By 1725, the natives were gone, leading to extensive European settlement beginning in 1726. The area became important for commerce after the British designated the Cape Fear River as one of the five official ports of entry to the colony. Sugarloaf, a fifty-foot sand dune nearby, was an important navigational marker for river traders. The area also hosted a Confederate camp during the Civil War. In 1969, Carolina Beach State Park was established to preserve a unique environment along the Cape Fear River and Snow's Cut. The area contains a sand dune, along with three sinkholes, rock outcrops made of shells and pocosins.

Jockey's Ridge State Park, Dare County

One of North Carolina's newer state parks, Jockey's Ridge is the largest active sand dune on the East Coast. There is almost no vegetation due to the changing winds. The winds blow from the southwest from March through August and from the northeast the rest of the year. The area was slated for development in 1973. Local citizens protested, and in 1975, the General Assembly created the Jockey's Ridge State Park. The park now contains 761 acres of places to explore.

Cape Hatteras National Seashore/Cape Lookout National Seashore

Stretching over seventy miles, from Bodie Island to Ocracoke Island, Cape Hatteras National Seashore overflows with natural and cultural history. The park was authorized in 1937 and, in 1953, became the first national seashore. There are three visitors' centers, located on Bodie Island, Hatteras Island and Ocracoke Island, as well as numerous museums, lifesaving stations and lighthouses. Continuing south from Ocracoke Island to Beaufort Island, travelers reach the Cape Lookout National Seashore. These barrier islands are largely undeveloped, containing North and South Core Banks and Shackleford Banks. There are also several historic areas, such as the Cape Lookout and Portsmouth Village Historic Districts.

Jockey's Ridge is the largest active sand dune in the eastern United States. Photo by Albert Barden, circa 1930–40. *State Archives of North Carolina.*

INNER COASTAL PLAIN

The coastal plain is the largest geographical area in North Carolina, covering about 45 percent of the state.

Great Dismal Swamp, Camden County

Spanning the states of North Carolina and Virginia, the Great Dismal Swamp is the largest remaining swamp in the eastern United States. There are more than two hundred species of birds, ninety-six species of butterflies, forty-seven species of mammals and 112,000 acres of contiguous forest. The Great Dismal Swamp also has a deep and interesting history. Native Americans hunted in the area. There were attempts to drain the swamp via canals to turn the area into farmland. Then came logging that removed

The Great Dismal Swamp has been visited by many over the years, including George Washington. *Photo by Albert Barden, State Archives of North Carolina.*

cypress and cedar trees. In the early 1700s came an idea to dig a canal from the Chesapeake Bay in Virginia to the Albemarle Sound. Work began in 1793, with most of the labor being performed by enslaved people. In 1805, the canal opened to small boat traffic. When the British blockaded the Chesapeake Bay during the War of 1812, the canal was used to transport supplies. Both Confederate and Union armies used the canal during the Civil War. The swamp also provided shelter for runaway slaves. Some stayed only a short time, while others made homes in the swamps. In 1974, the Great Dismal Swamp National Wildlife Refuge was officially established, with the North Carolina portion falling within the Dismal Swamp State Park. There is a visitors' center and a North Carolina Highway Historical Marker in South Mills.

Jones Lake State Park, Bladen County

On the border between the Tidewater and Inner Coastal Plain are thousands of oval-shaped depressions. They are known as the Carolina Bays. Characteristically, they are home to dense thickets of evergreen plants, lined with peat, with sandy shores. Many of them contain water. There are many theories about how these lakes were formed. Most geologists believe they are depressions created after the seas receded. Jones Lake is one of the Carolina Bays and was originally known as Woodward's Lake for early settler Samuel Woodward. The lake was renamed for Isaac Jones, a landowner who gave land for the establishment of nearby Elizabethtown, founded in 1773. After the demise of the turpentine, cotton and longleaf pine industries, the property was purchased by the federal government during the Great Depression and leased to North Carolina in 1939. Jones Lake became the first state park for African Americans in 1939. In 1954, ownership transferred to North Carolina.

Medoc Mountain State Park, Halifax County

The fall line in North Carolina is a boundary between the Piedmont and Inner Coastal Plain. Hard, erosion-resistant rocks characteristically found in the western portion of the state met softer rocks in the east. Medoc Mountain State Park lies along that fall line. At 325 feet above sea level, Medoc Mountain is not a very imposing mountain. But it once was a part of a large ridge. Time and millions of years of erosion have whittled down the rocks in the area. Sidney Weller cultivated grapes on the property in the 1840s. Weller's wine was named Weller's Halifax, and Weller is credited with developing grape and winemaking culture in the United States. Following Weller's death, the land was sold to the Garrett family, who named the property Medoc after a wine-producing region in France. A Boy Scout camp operated in the area in the 1920s, along with a dance hall, and later the property was often logged. At the bequest of local citizens, Medoc Mountain became a state park in the 1970s. There are numerous hiking trails, places to fish and camp and a visitors' center.

SANDHILLS

The Sandhill region stretches from North Carolina into South Carolina and Georgia. In North Carolina, parts of the counties of Cumberland, Harnett, Scotland, Richmond, Moore, Montgomery and Lee are in this area. The geology is composed of sand, sandstone and clay, and the vegetation is dominated by longleaf pines.

Weymouth Woods Sandhills Nature Preserve, Southern Pines

North Carolina was well known for its naval stores industry by the eighteenth century. The state produced turpentine, tar, pitch and rosin. Many choice trees were cut for the masts of Royal Navy ships. These industries took their toll on the state's forests. In 1903, James Boyd purchased several hundred acres of longleaf pine land to save them from logging. The property was donated to the State of North Carolina in 1963, preserving acres of longleaf pines dating back centuries. There are trees in the preserve from 250 to 450 years old, including one tree, dated to 1548, that is the oldest living longleaf pine in the world.

PIEDMONT

Beginning at an abrupt drop in elevation in the west at the Blue Ridge escarpment, the Piedmont is an area of gently rolling hills stretching east some 150 miles. The elevation drops from 1,500 feet to 300 feet.

Morrow Mountain State Park, Stanley County

Thousands of years ago, local inhabitants began quarrying stone to make tools at Morrow Mountain. The area, located in the Uwharrie Mountain Range, is one of the most extensive prehistoric quarries in the United States. Settlers moved into the area in the mid-1700s. John Kirk established a ferry here in 1780, carrying passengers and freight over the Pee Dee River on the Fayetteville to Salisbury Road. The ferry was in operation until a bridge downstream replaced it in the 1920s. Nearby is the ghost town of Tindallsville, which had a post office in 1799. The town might have been wiped out by a typhoid fever outbreak. Development of the Morrow Mountain State Park began in the 1930s, and it was opened to the public in 1939. The park visitors' center was constructed by the Civilian Conservation Corps in the 1930s. Camping, boating and numerous trails are also available. The home of Dr. Francis J. Kron, an early doctor and horticulturalist, has been restored.

FOOTHILLS AND MOUNTAINS

In a state already rich in biological and geographical diversity, the western part of North Carolina is hard to beat. The Blue Ridge Mountains in Western North Carolina are some of the oldest mountains in the world. They are a part of the Appalachians, which stretch from Newfoundland to Alabama. There are more than sixty peaks in North Carolina above six thousand feet in elevation, and there are more types of plants in the mountains than in any other area of comparable size in North America. Some areas still contain old-growth forests, more than in any other area in Southern Appalachia.

Mount Mitchell State Park, Yancey County

The Black Mountains are a fifteen-mile-long ridge with numerous peaks. Up until the 1850s, they were considered a single mountain. In the mid-1800s, the ridge came under the observation of Dr. Elisha Mitchell, professor of chemistry, geology and mineralogy. Mitchell was surveying various mountains in Western North Carolina. After climbing Grandfather Mountain, Mitchell was convinced that both Roan Mountain and Black Mountain were taller. Mitchell surveyed the Blacks in 1835, 1838 and 1844. Thomas L. Clingman, a U.S. congressman and former student of Dr. Mitchell's, was also out measuring mountain peaks. He believed that Mitchell had measured the wrong peak and that he himself had measured the correct peak as the tallest. Mitchell returned to the Blacks in 1857 to take additional measurements. On his way down the mountain, he slipped and fell to his death. When Mitchell did not return, locals spread out over the region to find him. Famed bear hunter Big Tom Wilson was credited with discovering Mitchell's body. Mitchell was buried on the top of the mountain, and in 1858, the highest point, not just in North Carolina but in the eastern United States, was named in his honor. Mitchell's measurement

Dr. Elisha Mitchell is buried on the mountain that bears his name. *Author's collection.*

of the tallest peak was 6,672 feet, just 12 feet from today's measurement of 6,684 feet. In 1915, Mount Mitchell became North Carolina's first state park. Mount Mitchell State Park, accessible from the Blue Ridge Parkway, has a visitors' center, museum and numerous hiking trails that explore the geology, geography and history of the area.

Grandfather Mountain, Avery County

When André Michaux climbed Grandfather Mountain in 1794, he thought he was on the tallest mountain in all of North America. At just 5,946 feet in elevation, Grandfather is far from the tallest. Yet the exposed rocks and breathtaking drop to the valley below could certainly give that impression. Beyond the geology of Grandfather Mountain, visitors can find one of the most biologically diverse places in the United States. Driving from the bottom to the top is a trip that covers more than sixteen distinct ecological communities. Botanists such as John Fraser, Asa Gray, John Muir and Emmett R. Dunn have explored the area. In 1992, the United Nations designated Grandfather Mountain as a Biosphere Reserve. Much of the mountain was acquired by the McRae family in the late 1800s. A grandson, Hugh Morton, developed part of the mountain as an attraction,

Grandfather Mountain is one of the most scenic and diverse locations in North Carolina. *Lees-McRae College Archives.*

with the world-famous Mile-High Swinging Bridge, a Nature Center and hiking trails. In 2008, the State of North Carolina acquired 2,456 acres of the mountain. The property became Grandfather Mountain State Park in 2009. The attraction side was transferred to the Grandfather Mountain Stewardship Foundation.

Linville Falls, McDowell County

The Cherokee called it Ee-see-oh, the "river of many cliffs." The Linville River, which has its origins in Avery County, cuts through the Blue Ridge Escarpment at Linville Falls. The river and falls (and other towns and places in the area) are named for a father and son killed by a group of "northern Indians" while hunting in the area in 1766. Later, the area was the site of a Confederate camp during the Civil War; then it became a popular tourist attraction with cabins and fishing guides. In 1952, John D. Rockefeller, at the bequest of local people, purchased the property and gave it to the National Park Service. It is now one of the most popular stops on the Blue

Ridge Parkway. There is a small visitors' center, campground and picnic area, along with numerous trails that lead to both the basin of the falls and overlooks above the falls.

Joyce Kilmer Memorial Forest, Graham County

Described as one of the most impressive old-growth forests in the United States, the Joyce Kilmer Memorial Forest has more than one hundred trees that are more than four hundred years old. The forest is 3,800 acres and was designated in 1936 as a memorial to Joyce Kilmer, author of the poem "Trees." Kilmer was killed in France during World War I.

Further Reading:

John Alexander and James Lazell, *Ribbon of Sand: The Amazing Convergence of the Ocean and the Outer Banks* (2000)

Timothy Silver, *Mount Mitchell and the Black Mountains* (2003)

Kevin G. Stewart and Mary-Russell Robertson, *Exploring the Geology of the Carolinas: A Field Guide to Favorite Places from Chimney Rock to Charleston* (2007)

FIRST NORTH CAROLINIANS

THE NATIVE AMERICANS

The history of Native Americans in North Carolina begins thousands of years prior to the arrival of European explorers and settlers. Paleoindians arrived in the state at the end of the last ice age (10,000–8000 BC). They hunted and gathered edible plants, living in small family groups. During the Archaic period (8000–1000 BC), these small groups of people lived semi-nomadic lifestyles, spending months in certain locations, hunting and gathering. Population increased due to abundant food and the development of new tools. The Woodland period (1000 BC–AD 1550) followed. These people settled along rivers and developed agriculture, planting beans, squash, pumpkins and maize. Pottery defined their culture, as did the bow and arrow. Within this same period came the Mississippian Indians (AD 700–1500). Due to the abundance of farmable land producing food and plentiful game, they developed large towns, sometimes with pyramidal mounds that served as the bases for temples and the homes of chiefs. Many of these towns were enclosed by palisade forts.

When the first European explorers arrived, they found three major tribes and many smaller groups of Native Americans. Those three major tribes were the Tuscaroras, Catawbas and Cherokees. The Tuscaroras lived in the coastal plains, the Catawbas in the Piedmont and the Cherokees in the far western mountains. Spanish explorers seeking gold in the mid-sixteenth century encountered Native Americans in the piedmont, foothills and mountains regions. The Spanish built six forts in the interior of present-day North Carolina, trying to extend Spain's control in North America. All of these forts were later razed by Native American tribes nearby. Disease and wars with European settlers soon decimated the Native Americans in North Carolina.

By 1800, most of the tribes were gone. Some Native American peoples relocated elsewhere. The Cherokees in the far western counties were the last organized group, and the majority were forcibly removed in 1838, setting out along the Trail of Tears to land in Oklahoma. Only a small remnant remained, hidden in the mountains. They would become the Eastern Band of the Cherokee Nation. In the twenty-first century, North Carolina is the state east of the Mississippi River that has the largest number of people who identify as Native Americans. There are eight recognized tribes in the state: the Coharies, the Eastern Band of the Cherokee Indians, the Haliwa-Saponis, the Lumbee Tribe of North Carolina, the Meherrins, the Sapponys, the Occaneechi Band of the Saponi Nation and the Waccamaw Siouans.

COASTAL

Indian Woods, Bertie County

In 1717, the Northern Tuscaroras, who did not participate in the Southern Tuscaroras' failed war against the colonists, signed a treaty and were placed on a reservation along the Roanoke River in Bertie County. The fifty-three-thousand-acre tract of land became known as Indian Woods. There was, however, continued friction between the settlers and natives. In the early 1760s, a portion of the few remaining Tuscaroras decided to move to New York and join the Iroquois Confederation. In return for help with financing the move, the Tuscaroras leased much of the reservation. In 1828, the remaining members of the tribe gave up their title to the land. Most of the families moved to other areas. There is a North Carolina Highway Historical Marker south of Windsor.

Frisco Native American Museum, Dare County

Established in 1987, the Frisco Native American Museum goes beyond the local tribes, such as the Croatans, and local history. The museum tells the story of many different tribes across the United States. Exhibit subjects include an original canoe found on the property, pottery, dolls, beadwork and the Code Talkers. Outside are nature trails, a re-creation longhouse and fishing demonstrations.

PIEDMONT

Town Creek Indian Mound, Montgomery County

Two hundred years before European arrival, a group of Pee Dee Indians chose a spot on the Little River for a ceremonial center. While the site had seen previous occupation, the new residents constructed a mound with a temple and housing for high-ranking members of the tribe, along with burials of significance. The site was abandoned by Native Americans in colonial times. Excavations at Town Creek have been conducted since 1927. Landowners donated the property to the state in 1937, making the area the first state historic site. The site has an outstanding museum with a film and artifacts; the palisade walls, mound, temple and a few other structures have been rebuilt. Archaeological excavations are still conducted on a limited basis.

Town Creek was occupied by the Pee Dee Indians and became the first officially designated historic site in North Carolina. *Author's collection.*

Hardaway Site, Stanley County

About ten thousand years ago, a small group of people set up camp on a ridge near Badin, on the Yadkin River. They were followed by others, drawn to the rocks that were useful in manufacturing stone tools. These early peoples left behind a rich archaeological site. Identified by an amateur archaeologist in 1937 and then professionally excavated in 1948, the Hardaway site pushed back the date of first occupation in the eastern United States. Alcoa, which owns the property, donated 1.3 million artifacts from the site to the University of North Carolina in 2005. The Hardaway Site was declared a National Historic Landmark in 1990. A North Carolina Highway Historical Marker is in Badin.

Rural Heritage Center/Indian Museum of the Carolinas, Scotland County

Situated in the Sandhills region, the Indian Museum of the Carolinas largely focuses on the native tribes in a nine-county area surrounding Scotland County. This area includes the Lumbee Tribe, recognized by the State of North Carolina in 1885 and partially recognized by the federal government in 1956. As of 2021, the Lumbee Tribe is still struggling for full federal recognition. The Lumbees are the largest tribe in North Carolina, the largest east of the Mississippi River and the ninth-largest Native American tribe in the United States. The Indian Museum of the Carolinas works to tell the story of the Lumbees and their predecessors in the Sandhills area.

Museum of the Southeastern American Indian, Robeson County

The University of North Carolina–Pembroke has an interesting history. Local Native Americans had petitioned the General Assembly for a school in the area, and the General Assembly established the Croatan Normal School in 1887. In 1888, the school opened with one teacher and fifteen students. In 1919, the name was changed to the Indian Normal School of Robeson County and, in 1913, to the Cherokee Indian Normal School of Robeson County. A two-year teacher's program was added in 1926, followed by a junior college in 1933. In 1939, the school began offering four-year degrees, and in 1941, the name was changed to Pembroke State College for Indians.

Other changes followed: non-teaching baccalaureate degrees were added in 1943, followed by the admission of non-natives in 1945. The name was changed to Pembroke State College in 1949 and, in 1969, to the Pembroke State University. Students were granted admission regardless of ethnicity beginning in 1954. In 1996, the school officially became the University of North Carolina–Pembroke. Located in the Old Main Building on campus, the Museum of the Southeast American Indian's mission is to research and preserve the culture of Native Americans in Robeson County and the southeastern United States. The museum displays textiles and artifacts related to local native culture. There are North Carolina Highway Historical Markers for both the Croatan Normal School and the University of North Carolina–Pembroke in Pembroke.

Catawba Indian Reservation, Mecklenburg County

The Catawbas were identified as being one of the three major present-day North Carolina tribes present at the time of European settlement. Their homeland stretched from the headwaters of the Catawba River south though the central portion of the state. They called themselves yeh is-WAH h'reh, the "people of the river." Disease, war, political infighting and the encroachment of settlers wreaked havoc with the tribe during the colonial period. The government of South Carolina induced the remnants of the tribe to relocate to their state. In 1760 and 1763, the Catawbas negotiated a treaty establishing a reservation of some 144,000 acres. There is a North Carolina Highway Historical Marker denoting a portion of that original boundary in Pineville.

MOUNTAINS

Fort San Juan, Burke County

When Spanish explorers arrived in the foothills of the Blue Ridge Mountains, they found a robust Native American population living in a town called Joara. The Native Americans living at Joara are considered members of the late Mississippian culture. Hernando de Soto is believed to have visited the site in 1540. He quickly moved on, heading over the Blue Ridge Mountains and then west. In 1567, an expedition under the command of Juan Pardo arrived and constructed Fort San Juan, the first European settlement in the interior of North America. It was one of six forts built by the Spanish in what became North Carolina. The other forts were to the east of Fort San Juan. Eighteen months later, the Indians rose up and killed all but one of the Spanish, burning Fort San Juan in the process. The locations of the town and the fort were rediscovered by archaeologists, officially announced in 2013, and the site has ongoing archaeological excavations. While the site is open to the public once a year, the History Museum of Burke County, in nearby Morganton, has exhibits on the area.

Judaculla Rock, Jackson County

The Cherokees believe that a dreadful giant, Judaculla, made multiple carvings on a large soapstone boulder outside the town of Cullowhee. Other theories are that the markings, which predate Cherokee history, commemorate a peace treaty, a battle or possibly a boundary marker. The actual meanings of the petroglyphs are unknown. The Judaculla Rock is open to the public. There is a North Carolina Highway Historical Marker nearby.

The Judaculla Rock is the most impressive petroglyph in North Carolina. *Author's collection.*

The Museum of the Cherokee Indian, Cherokee County

Following the Indian Removal Act of 1830, a small band of Cherokees remained hidden in the mountains of Western North Carolina. William Holland Thomas, a white man who operated a store in Qualla, was adopted by Principal Chief Yonaguska. After the removal, Thomas, because of his support of those who remained behind, was made chief. Thomas argued vigorously for the legal claims of the Cherokees and purchased land, some fifty thousand acres, which formed the major portion of the Qualla Boundary. In 1866, members of the Eastern Band of the Cherokee were granted freedom to live in North Carolina, and in 1874, the land that Thomas had purchased was placed in a trust for the Cherokees who lived in the area. Their seat of government is located in Cherokee, also the location of the Museum of the Cherokee Indian. The museum was created in 1948 and houses the greatest

Opening in 1950, *Unto These Hills* is the third-oldest outdoor historical drama in the United States. *Iredell County Public Library.*

collection of Cherokee artifacts in the world. Nearby is the Oconaluftee Indian Village, which takes visitors back to the eighteenth century, prior to removal. Likewise, the *Unto These Hills* outdoor drama portrays the history of the Cherokees from 1780 to the present.

Junaluska Memorial Site, Robbinsville, Graham County

Although not a chief, Junaluska played an important part in the history of Cherokees and the United States. When the Shawnees wanted the Cherokees to join them in fighting against settlers, Junaluska led a party that refused. Instead, he led a group of warriors to join the United States in fighting against the Creeks in 1813. According to popular culture, Junaluska saved Andrew Jackson's life during the Battle of Horseshoe Bend, a decision that Junaluska regretted following the passage of the Indian Removal Act of 1830. Junaluska survived the Trail of Tears but, after losing most of his family, walked back to North Carolina. In 1847, the North Carolina General Assembly granted Junaluska 337 acres of land, $100 and citizenship in recognition of his military service. The Junaluska Memorial marks his grave in Robbinsville, and there is a North Carolina Highway Historical Marker nearby.

Further Reading:

David La Vere, *The Tuscarora War: Indians, Settlers, and the Fight for the Carolina Colonies* (2016)

E. Lawrence Lee, *Indian Wars in North Carolina, 1663–1763* (1963, 2011)

Theda Purdue, *Native Carolinians: The Indians of North Carolina* (2017)

THE GOLDEN AGE OF PIRACY

Stede Bonnet, William Lewis, Charles Vane, Anne Bonny, Mary Read, Black Caesar and Blackbeard are just a few of the notorious pirates who once roamed the coast of North Carolina. The Golden Age of Piracy stretched from 1689 to 1718. One historian estimated that in 1717, there were two thousand pirates lurking off the coast of North Carolina. They found the shallow waters of the Pamlico and Albemarle Sounds and the Cape Fear River easy places to hide from large British warships patrolling the area. They also sought ships following the current from Central America up the North American coast. These ships often carried sugar, tobacco, cocoa and even slaves. Weapons (such as cannons), rigging and sails for ships were often taken, and at times, the entire ship was confiscated. Some ships were burned, while others became a part of a pirate flotilla or were disassembled to repair other vessels.

Born in New York around 1655, William Kidd obtained a license from King William to attack French shipping in August 1695. Great Britain and France were at war. Becoming a privateer could be very lucrative. Captain Kidd was back in America in May 1696, and by September, his ship, the *Adventure Galley*, was cruising, looking for targets. Kidd ran into various problems, including being labeled a pirate by the Royal Navy and conflicts with one of his crew, whom he later killed with a wooden bucket. The *Adventure Galley* soon proved unseaworthy, and Kidd moved his crew onto one of the two ships he had captured. However, part of his crew mutinied. Kidd set sail toward New York. He supposedly, in 1699, buried part of his loot on

Money Island, near Wrightsville Beach. In New York, he was arrested and sent to London, where he was tried as a pirate. A sham trial was held, and Kidd was found guilty. He was hanged on May 23, 1701.

Stede Bonnet, the "Gentleman Pirate," was not a typical swashbuckler. He was educated and came from a well-to-do Barbados family. What drove him into piracy remains a mystery, although several accounts blame marital discord. In 1717, Bonnet also went so far as to purchase a ship, the *Revenge*, and hire a crew, setting sail toward the coast of New York. It was probably September when he sailed into the Cape Fear River to careen and repair his ship. In the Bay of Honduras, Bonnet ran into Blackbeard and *Queen Anne's Revenge*. They agreed to sail together, and Bonnet actually transferred to Blackbeard's ship, enjoying a life of ease. By the time they reached Topsail Island in June 1718, Blackbeard was commanding four ships and four hundred pirates. With dissention rife among so many pirates, Blackbeard transferred command of the *Revenge* back to Bonnet. Bonnet then sailed to Bath to gain a pardon from Governor Charles Eden. When he returned, he discovered Blackbeard gone with the loot. Bonnet's attempt to follow Blackbeard up the coast was unsuccessful. Adopting an alias and renaming his ship, Bonnet attempted to fool the government, returning to piracy. While careening the ship in the Cape Fear River in September 1718, the pirates were discovered by two pirate-hunting sloops out of South Carolina. In the ensuing battle, Bonnet was captured, taken to Charleston and hanged on December 10, 1718.

"Calico Jack" Rackham not only had a colorful name, but he also kept colorful company. Rackham sailed with Charles Vane in 1718, and when the crew voted Vane off the ship, Calico Jack was elected captain. It was a common occurrence for pirate crews to elect their commanders. Like many other pirates, he applied for clemency under the "Proclamation for Suppressing Pirates" in 1717 that absolved pirates of their crimes if they simply applied. At Nassau, he met Anne Bonny (Bonney), the wife of pirate James Bonny. Anne Bonny supposedly grew up in North Carolina. Calico Jack and Anne Bonny set sail together in August 1719. Among the crew was Mary Reade, a British soldier's widow who signed aboard as a seaman. As the story goes, Anne and Mary would dress like women until a target sailed into view, and then they changed into men's clothing. They were eventually captured off Jamaica. Calico Jack was hanged on November 27, 1720. Anne and Mary were both condemned to the same fate. Both, however, claimed to be pregnant and were not executed. Mary died in a Jamaican prison in 1721, and Anne disappeared from the pages of history.

Anne Bonny (*left*) and Mary Reade are believed to have sailed as pirates with Calico Jack in 1719. *State Archives of North Carolina.*

Charles Vane declined a pardon when issued and dramatically sailed out of Nassau in July 1718, heading for the North American coast. He plied the waters between Florida and New York. Vane was known for his cruelty, often torturing prisoners. Vane took eight ships near the entrance to Charleston, which led South Carolina merchants to outfit two sloops to hunt him. Vane was rumored to be near the Cape Fear River, but the pirate hunters found Stede Bonnet instead. In September, Vane was reported to have met Blackbeard at Ocracoke Inlet. Vane refused to attack a French naval frigate in November, which led to his being replaced by Calico Jack. Vane and the crew of one of his ships were shipwrecked in February 1719. When a British naval vessel arrived to collect water, Vane was recognized, arrested and taken to Jamaica, where he was tried, found guilty and hanged on March 29, 1721.

Edward Teach, Edward Thatch, Edward Drummond or maybe just Blackbeard—whatever he might have been called, he was the most feared and highly romanticized pirate in history. Just as we are uncertain of his name, we are also uncertain of where he was born. Jamaica or Bristol, England, are two popular possible sites for his birth, but Philadelphia and

Blackbeard, the most famous pirate of all time, was killed fighting off Ocracoke Island in 1718. *Library of Congress.*

North Carolina are also suggested. It is believed that he sailed first on a ship transporting slaves from Africa to the Bahamas and then later as a privateer during Queen Anne's War. When the opportunity for privateering ended in 1713, he probably signed on with Captain Benjamin Hornigold as a pirate. After capturing a French prize, Hornigold made Teach captain, rechristening the vessel the *Queen Anne's Revenge.* Hornigold soon accepted the king's pardon, parting ways with Teach. At some point, Teach, because of his long black beard, became known as Blackbeard. He tied his beard up with ribbons, stuck lighted fuses under his hat and built a fearsome reputation. The reputations that pirates fostered often allowed them to capture ships without fighting.

In May 1718, Blackbeard and his flotilla of ships blockaded the port of Charleston. Up to nine vessels were captured, and the pirates demanded payment from the town. The payment included a chest full of medicine.

By June 3, Blackbeard had arrived at Topsail Island, and around June 10, the *Queen Anne's Revenge* ran aground near Beaufort. He stripped the vessels and marooned 250 pirates as he headed to Bath to get a pardon for his evil ways. As the legend goes, upon obtaining a pardon, he moved into a house in Bath and married a local girl. He kept another vessel, the *Adventure*, in Ocracoke, along with a selected number of crewmen. At the end of August, Blackbeard was on his way to Bermuda, capturing five ships. He returned to Bath and claimed that one of the ships was found with no crew, which the courts accepted. The cargo was unloaded, and the ship was burned. Hearing the news that Blackbeard was using the Ocracoke area as a base, Governor Alexander Spotswood of Virginia quickly commissioned two small sloops to track down the pirate, all without notifying Governor Eden of North Carolina that he was entering that colony's waters. This military foray also included a land force. The naval portion was under the command of Lieutenant Robert Maynard.

On the evening of November 21, Maynard found the *Adventure* near Ocracoke Island. The next morning, he attacked. His two sloops had no cannons. One sloop grounded on a sandbar early and played little role in the battle. Maynard hid most of his men in the hold of his ship. When the pirates swung on board, the men quickly swarmed out of the hold. Maynard and Blackbeard faced off, and with the help of another sailor, Maynard was able to kill Blackbeard. He later noted that the pirate had been shot five times and slashed twenty. Overall, eight sailors and twelve pirates were killed. Those captured were taken to Virginia, tried and executed. Blackbeard's head was hung from one of Maynard's ships and his body dumped overboard. While piracy did not end with the death of Blackbeard, increased pressure by the British navy rooted out many of the pirates.

Black Caesar was one of many Black crewmen who served with Blackbeard as full members of his crew. When a captured ship was transporting slaves, they were sometimes given the option of joining pirate crews. Black Caesar was in the hold of the *Adventure* when the battle took place, charged with blowing up the powder magazine should the ship be captured. He was overpowered before he could complete his task, taken to Virginia, tried with the other crewmembers and executed.

There are several sites associated with North Carolina's pirate history. North Carolina Highway Trail Markers for Edward Teach are located in Bath (Beaufort County) and Ocracoke Island at the Cedar Island ferry landing (Carteret County); one dedicated to Lieutenant Robert Maynard is at the Ocracoke ferry landing (Hyde County).

Queen Anne's Revenge was discovered in November 1996 near Beaufort Inlet. The wreck was in the right place for the identification, and over time, more evidence has emerged, leading to a largely accepted consensus that this was indeed Blackbeard's flagship. While preservation work is ongoing, many of the conserved objects can be found at the North Carolina Maritime Museum in Beaufort, while smaller collections can be found at the North Carolina Maritime Museum in Southport and the North Carolina Museum of History in Raleigh.

French pirate Jean Lafitte came one hundred years after the Golden Age of Piracy. He operated in the Gulf of Mexico in the early nineteenth century. Lafitte supposedly faked his own death and moved to present-day Lincoln County. He died circa 1823 and is buried at St. Luke's Episcopal Church in Lincolnton, under the name of Lorenzo Ferrer.

Further Reading:

Lindley Butler, *Pirates, Privateers, and Rebel Raiders of the Carolina Coast* (2000)
Angus Konstam, *Blackbeard: America's Most Notorious Pirate* (2007)
Hugh Rankin, *The Pirates of Colonial North Carolina* (2010)

THE GRAVEYARD OF THE ATLANTIC

NORTH CAROLINA SHIPWRECKS

Legend has it that Founding Father Alexander Hamilton coined the term "Graveyard of the Atlantic." That might be a tall tale, as might be the idea that more than five thousand ships have been lost along North Carolina's Outer Banks. Regardless, there have been hundreds of documented ships lost on the Diamond, Lookout and Frying Pan Shoals. Some of the most famed are honored with markers, memorials and museum exhibits.

SS *PEVENSEY*, CARTERET COUNTY

Blockade runners were crucial to the Southern war effort during the 1860s. They brought in vital supplies that supported the Confederate armies. Many of these vessels were shallow-draft and steam powered. The SS *Pevensey* was an iron-hulled sidewheel steamer with one deck and two masts. It was built in London in 1863 or early 1864. The *Pevensey* made several runs into Wilmington before June 9, 1864, when it was driven ashore at Pine Knoll Shores and blown up. Parts of the wreck are occasionally visible at low tide. A North Carolina Highway Historical Marker is located in Pine Knoll Shores.

USS *Monitor*, Dare County

Revolutionary for the time, the USS *Monitor* was not exactly seaworthy despite its role in the well-known "duel of the ironclads" with the CSS *Virginia* (the rechristened USS *Merrimack*). Constructed with a low water line, the ironclad ship leaked when the seas washed over it. After the port of Norfolk was captured, the *Monitor* was no longer needed in Hampton Roads, and while it was being towed to Charleston to participate in an attack, it was swamped off Cape Hatteras and went down in 230 feet of water, taking sixteen members of the crew with it. Portions of the ship were found in 1973, and in 2002, the turret was raised and is currently under conservation at a museum in Virginia. There is a North Carolina Highway Historical Marker at Hatteras.

Diamond Shoals, Dare County

During both of the world wars, German submarines found the North Carolina coast a rich opportunity for sinking vessels. In May 1918, *U-151* arrived off the Outer Banks, attacking supply vessels and laying mines at harbor entrances. By the time of the armistice in November 1918, it had sunk thirty-four ships and damaged seven others. Within three weeks of the United States entering World War II, German U-boats were again attacking shipping along the East Coast. In a four-month period, almost seventy ships were sunk along the North Carolina coast. By mid-1942, the United States was fighting back with sheltered harbors, mine fields and patrol ships and planes. Overall, U.S. forces sank at least four U-boats off North Carolina before the war ended. A North Carolina Highway Historical Marker commemorating the action is in Buxton.

USS *Huron*, Dare County

Commissioned in Philadelphia in 1875, the iron-hulled screw steamer *Huron* was a U.S. Navy gunboat. It cruised the Caribbean and the Gulf of Mexico. On a cruise from Hampton Roads toward Cuba, it ran aground in a storm off Nags Head on November 23, 1877. Out of 133 crew members, 83 sailors went down with the ship. The tragedy led to an expansion of lifesaving stations up and down the coast. A North Carolina Highway Historical Marker commemorating the ship is located in Nags Head.

After its famous duel with the CSS *Virginia*, the USS *Monitor* sank off Cape Hatteras in a storm. *U.S. Naval History and Heritage Command Photograph.*

The USS *Huron* sank in 1877 off Nags Head, losing 83 out of 133 on board. *U.S. Naval History and Heritage Command Photograph.*

Mirlo Rescue, Dare County

The British petroleum tanker *Mirlo* was a casualty of a German mine on August 10, 1918. The crew of fifty-two men abandoned ship, but the gasoline leaking out of the ship soon caught the ocean on fire. The brave Coast Guard men from the Chicamacomico Coast Guard Station rescued forty-two of the British sailors. There is a North Carolina Highway Historical Marker located in Salvo.

Wreck of the *Metropolis*, Currituck County

The *Metropolis* was much older than its owners revealed when it was chartered to transport 245 workers from Philadelphia to Brazil in 1878. Instead of being just a few years old, as claimed, it was actually built in 1861 and originally named *The Stars and Stripes.* As the vessel sailed by the beach at Currituck, it was leaking badly, struck the shoals and began to sink; 85 of the

Eighty-five people perished when the *Metropolis* sank off Currituck in 1878. *Library of Congress.*

passengers died in the wreck. The sinking of this vessel, along with the USS *Huron*, led to changes in the lifesaving stations. There is a North Carolina Highway Historical Marker in Corolla near the site of the sinking.

CONDOR, NEW HANOVER COUNTY

There were scores of ships lost along the coast during the Civil War. In the Cape Fear area, there are twenty-one vessels listed. One of those is about seven hundred yards east of Fort Fisher. The *Condor* was an ordinary blockade runner, except for one passenger: the famed Confederate spy Rose O'Neal Greenhow. Living in Washington, D.C., at the beginning of the war, Greenhow was able to spy on Federal troop movements. This led to her arrest and incarceration. After her release, she sailed for France and Great Britain, raising money for the Confederate cause. Upon her return in August 1864, her ship, the *Condor*, was chased by Union ships and ran aground. Insisting that she be taken ashore, she boarded a rowboat that later capsized. Weighted down by gold sewn into her skirt, she drowned and was interred at Oakdale Cemetery in Wilmington. There are, at times, buoys marking the wreck site off Fort Fisher.

North Carolina has three state museums that focus on the state's maritime history. These include the North Carolina Maritime Museum in Beaufort, the North Carolina Maritime Museum in Southport and the Graveyard of the Atlantic Museum/North Carolina Maritime Museum in Hatteras. There are also many local museums along the coast that have maritime displays.

Further Reading:

David Stick, *Graveyard of the Atlantic: Shipwrecks of the North Carolina Coast* (1952)

LIGHTHOUSES AND LIFESAVING STATIONS

North Carolina has 301 miles of shoreline. Lighthouses are built to serve as navigational aids and warn mariners of dangerous areas. Considering the thousands of shipwrecks off the North Carolina coast, there are plenty of dangerous areas, like Frying Pan Shoals and Diamond Shoals. Many of these areas have used lighthouses to warn ships. Listed here are only existing lighthouses. Some of those that no longer exist are the Campbell Island Lighthouse, New Hanover County, destroyed in 1865; Cape Fear Light, New Hanover County, demolished in 1958; Croatan Shoal Light, Croatan Sound, destroyed in 1864; Diamond Shoal Light, offshore, inactive since 2001; Federal Point Light, New Hanover County, destroyed in 1881; Frying Pan Shoals light, offshore, inactive since 2003; Gulf Shoal Light, Pamlico Sound, destroyed on an unknown date; Hatteras Beacon, Dare County, removed in 1898; Laurel Point Light, Tyrell County, demolished in the 1950s; Long Point Beacon Light, Tyrell County, destroyed on an unknown date; Neuse River Light, Pamlico County, destroyed on an unknown date; North River Light, Currituck/Camden Counties, moved in 1920; Pamlico Point Light Shoal, Pamlico County, demolished in the 1950s; Price Creek Light, Brunswick County, inactive since 1865; Roanoke Marshes Light, Dare County, destroyed in 1955; and Wade Point Light, Camden and Pasquotank Counties, destroyed in the 1950s. There is a reproduction of the Roanoke Marshes Light in the town of Manteo on Shallowbag Bay.

BALD HEAD "OLD BALDY" LIGHTHOUSE, BRUNSWICK COUNTY

The oldest standing lighthouse in North Carolina, Old Baldy has been guiding ships into the Cape Fear River and away from Frying Pan Shoals since 1818. This was the second lighthouse constructed on Bald Head Island and is one of the few surviving Federal-style octagonal lighthouses in the United States. During the Civil War, Confederate forces removed the lights and built Fort Holmes around the lighthouse. Old Baldy was decommissioned in 1866 but was relit in 1880, only to be deactivated in 1935. It did serve as a radio beacon during World War II. Today, the lighthouse is maintained by the Old Baldy Foundation, which has restored the lighthouse and reconstructed the lightkeeper's house. The structures are open to the public. A North Carolina Highway Historical Marker is located in Southport.

"Old Baldy" is the oldest standing lighthouse in North Carolina. *State Archives of North Carolina.*

BODIE ISLAND LIGHTHOUSE, DARE COUNTY

While there had been numerous recommendations to construct a light on Bodie Island, near the Diamond Shoals, it was not until 1837 that Congress appropriated the funds, and it was not until 1847 that the light was completed. Because of a poor foundation, the light was abandoned in 1858. A second tower was completed in 1858 but was destroyed during the Civil War. Due to the changing geography, both of the original sites are now underwater. Standing at 167 feet in height, the third and current tower was completed in 1872. The property was transferred to the National Park Service in 1953. The Bodie Island Lighthouse is open for tours.

OCRACOKE LIGHTHOUSE, HYDE COUNTY

Originally, at the end of the eighteenth century, a lighthouse was built on Shell Castle Island for Ocracoke Inlet. This station was destroyed by lightning in 1818. A new tower was constructed on Ocracoke Island. Completed in 1823, it stood sixty-five feet tall. During the Civil War, Confederate forces removed the lens, but in 1863, with the island under Union control, a new lens was installed. Upgrades to the lighthouse were made through the next few decades. During World War II, the tower served as a lookout for Coast Guard personnel. A small cemetery is nearby for British sailors who died when German U-boats sank their ships. In 1999, ownership of the Ocracoke Lighthouse transferred from the U.S. Coast Guard to the National Park Service. The Ocracoke Lighthouse is the second-oldest operating lighthouse in the nation. The grounds are open for visitors. A North Carolina Highway Historical Marker is located nearby.

CAPE HATTERAS LIGHTHOUSE, DARE COUNTY

The first lighthouse at Cape Hatteras was 90 feet tall and in operation by October 1803. In the 1850s, the lighthouse's height was extended another 60 feet, and it was painted red and white. During the Civil War, the lens was removed and shipped inland. The lens was returned in 1870, when the second Cape Hatteras Lighthouse was completed. The new tower was 189 feet tall. Erosion has always been a major issue for the Cape Hatteras Light. The light was decommissioned in 1935 and moved to a skeletal steel

The keeper's house and Cape Hatteras Lighthouse were relocated, along with other structures, in 1999, ten years after this photo was taken. *Library of Congress.*

tower a mile away. The property transferred to the National Park Service in 1937. In 1950, the Coast Guard was able to relight the lighthouse. Work had gone into shoring up the beach area near the lighthouse. However, erosion continued to be a problem. In 1999, the lighthouse, keeper's quarters, oil house and dwelling cisterns were all relocated 2,900 feet from their original location. The Cape Hatteras Lighthouse is open seasonally for tours. A North Carolina Highway Historical Marker is located in Buxton.

CAPE LOOKOUT LIGHTHOUSE, CARTERET COUNTY

Every lighthouse has a different paint scheme. The Cape Lookout Lighthouse bears the distinctive black-and-white diamond paint pattern. The original Cape Lookout light was not tall enough, and the light was dim. This tower, operational by 1812, was replaced in 1859. As was the case with the other lighthouses along the coast, the lenses were removed by the Confederates in 1861. Union troops captured the area in 1862, and by the next year, a new lens was installed. There was an attempt to blow up the lighthouse by Confederate forces in 1864. In 2003, the Cape Lookout Lighthouse was transferred to the National Park Service. There is a museum near the lighthouse and a North Carolina Highway Historical Marker nearby.

CURRITUCK BEACH LIGHTHOUSE, CURRITUCK COUNTY

While the project was originally proposed in the mid-1850s, it was not until 1876 that the Currituck Beach Light was completed. The tower is 162 feet and unpainted and was the last brick lighthouse constructed on the Outer Banks. During World War I, the keepers watched for German submarines. In 1939, the lighthouse was automated and transferred to the U.S. Coast Guard. During World War II, the Coast Guard used horses to patrol the beaches. Stables were built nearby, and the lightkeeper's house was used to store hay. In October 2003, the deed of the lighthouse was transferred to the Outer Banks Conservationists Inc., which restored the lighthouse and some of the buildings. The lighthouse is open from Easter through Thanksgiving.

OAK ISLAND LIGHTHOUSE, BRUNSWICK COUNTY

Constructed in 1958, the Oak Island Lighthouse was the last lighthouse built along the North Carolina coast. At 153 feet, it provides guidance into the Cape Fear River. The property is owned by the Town of Caswell Beach, and the light is maintained by the U.S. Coast Guard. Restoration work is provided by the Friends of Oak Island Lighthouse. Tours are offered by reservation and are usually available on Wednesdays and Saturdays.

ROANOKE RIVER LIGHT, CHOWAN COUNTY

At one time, North Carolina had several interior barrier island light stations. The only surviving example is the Roanoke River Light. Constructed in 1866–67 near the confluence of the Roanoke River and the Albemarle Sound, this light replaced a light vessel destroyed during the Civil War. The station was destroyed by fire and rebuilt in 1885. The light station has been moved twice, restored and currently resides on the waterfront in Edenton.

Constructed in 1958, the Oak Island Lighthouse is the newest lighthouse in North Carolina. *Michael C. Hardy.*

LIFESAVING STATIONS

With such dangerous shoals off the coast leading to countless shipwrecks, North Carolina eventually had twenty-nine lifesaving stations, averaging about six miles apart. The stations were manned from late spring to early fall by a keeper and a crew of six men. The first stations formed in North Carolina in 1874 were at Jones Hill, Caffey's Inlet, Kitty Hawk, Nags Head, Bodie Island, Chicamacomico and Little Kinnakeet. The crew of each station was responsible for patrolling a section of beach and sea for grounded or stranded vessels. When a lifesaver located a stranded vessel, he lit flares and headed back to collect the others and the equipment. At times the lifesaver fired a line from a Lyle gun, a small cannon, to the ship. If successful, the larger line was run out, and a breeches buoy used to bring the passengers from ship to shore. If the vessel was too far out, then a surfboat was launched and rowed to the ship. Often, ships were driven aground by storms, and the surfboats had to navigate through the breakers to reach the

The Kill Devil Hills Life-Saving Station, with four members of the lifesaving crew and their boats, circa 1902, was a typical early twentieth-century installation. *Library of Congress.*

stranded crews. Later, a few of the stations had powerboats. In 1915, the U.S. Life-Saving Service was combined with the Revenue Cutter Service to form the U.S. Coast Guard, and the Coast Guard assumed the responsibility for the lifesaving stations.

Bodie Island Life-Saving Station, Dare County

The original Bodie Island Life-Saving Station was constructed south of Oregon Inlet in 1874 on Pea Island. In 1878, a station was built just above the Bodie Island Lighthouse and named Tommy's Hummock Life-Saving Station. In 1883, the names were changed. Tommy's Hummock became the Bodie Island station, and the old Bodie Island station became the Oregon Inlet station. Eventually, the keeper's house and a 1903 boathouse were transferred to the National Park Service and moved to the entrance of the Bodie Island Lighthouse.

Chicamacomico Life-Saving Station Historic Site, Dare County

Established in 1874, the Chicamacomico Life-Saving Station was one of the first built in North Carolina. This station helped rescue sailors from the *Mirlo* in 1918. With numerous original buildings, it is also one of the most

Kinnakeet Life-Saving Station, circa 1893–99, was one of the earliest lifesaving stations in the state. *State Archives of North Carolina.*

complete lifesaving stations in the United States. The site also contains a self-bailing motor surfboat, cook house, water towers, stable and other rescue equipment.

Further Reading:

Joe A. Mobley, *Ship Ashore!: The U.S. Lifesavers of Coastal North Carolina* (1994)

Cheryl Shelton-Roberts and Bruce Roberts, *North Carolina Lighthouses* (2019)

EXPLORERS AND NATURALISTS

When the first European explorers arrived in the sixteenth century, they found a vast wilderness of trees, rivers, sandhills and mountains. Native Americans inhabited selected spots along the banks and shorelines of many streams and lakes. The Spanish were the first to explore deeply into the wilderness, followed by the English, French and Germans. Ships soon arrived, bearing settlers. They pushed out the natives, establishing towns modeled on those they left behind in the Old World, often on the sites of villages built by natives. Not long after the explorers came, naturalists and botanists followed, discovering species of flora and fauna wildly divergent from those they had observed back in the Old World.

COASTAL

Verrazzano, Carteret County

There were several Europeans who probably sailed within sight of the Outer Banks early in the sixteenth century. These include Pedro de Quejo and Lucas Vázquez de Ayllón, both employed in capturing people for enslavement. Florentine explorer Giovanni da Verrazzano arrived in 1524, exploring the Cape Fear River area. Verrazzano believed that he had found a shorter route to the Orient. In Pine Knoll Shore, there is a North Carolina Highway Historical Marker that mentions Verrazzano.

Lane's Expedition, Hertford County

Sir Ralph Lane left England with 107 colonists in 1585. They arrived off Ocracoke two months later, establishing a colony, and Lane was named governor. The group later moved to Roanoke Island and established Fort Raleigh, while also exploring the Chesapeake Bay and Chowan River areas. A year later, the group abandoned their efforts and sailed back to England. A North Carolina Highway Historical Marker can be found in Hertford County.

Fort Raleigh National Historic Site, Dare County

In 1587, a group of colonists arrived on Roanoke Island. They occupied Fort Raleigh and made necessary repairs. The colony was plagued by a lack of supplies, and their leader, John White, returned to England to procure necessary items. The Anglo-Spanish War prevented White from returning until 1590. When he did return, he discovered the colony abandoned. Found carved on a tree was the word *Croatoan*. White believed this clue meant that the colonists had moved to nearby Croatoan Island. However, the fates of the colonists, along with Virginia Dare, the first English child born in North America, remain a mystery to this day. Fort Raleigh National Historic Site was established in 1941 and was listed in the National Register of Historic Places in 1966. Besides ruins that may be of the fort, there is a visitors' center, the Elizabethan Gardens and the Waterside Theater, where Paul Green's outdoor drama, *The Lost Colony*, has been performed since 1937. There are North Carolina Highway Historical Markers on the first English colonies and Virginia Dare located north of Manteo.

John Lawson, Pitt County

Born in Yorkshire, John Lawson was a trained scientist who sailed to the colonies in 1700. He journeyed through the Carolinas, recording the topography, Native Americans, flora and fauna that he encountered. His journals, published in 1709 and entitled *A New Voyage to Carolina*, have been heralded as the most comprehensive account of Native American culture and natural history written prior to the American Revolution. Later, Lawson

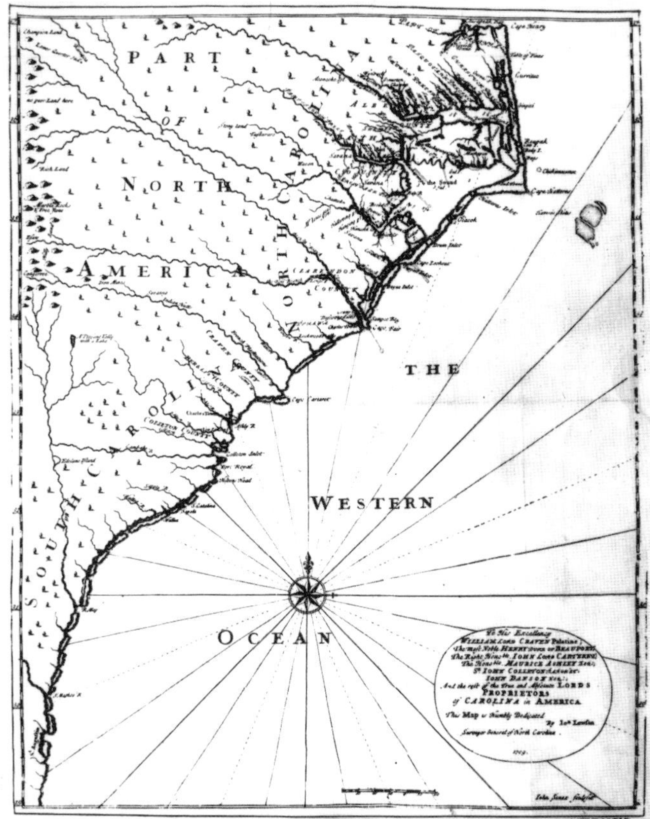

Top: Fort Raleigh, on Roanoke Island, was built in the latter part of the sixteenth century and became a National Historic Site in 1941. *Library of Congress.*

Bottom: This map appeared in John Lawson's book chronicling his travels through the Carolinas in 1709. *State Archives of North Carolina.*

was commissioned as North Carolina's first surveyor general, charged with finding the border between North Carolina and Virginia. In 1711, Lawson was ambushed and killed by a band of Tuscarora Indians while trying to find the source of the Neuse River. A North Carolina Highway Trail Marker is located near the site of his death in Grifton.

PIEDMONT

John Lederer, Vance County

Between May and July 1670, German native Dr. John Lederer explored the Carolina Piedmont. His goal was to find a passage through the Appalachian Mountains. Lederer left descriptions of the topography and natives he encountered. However, his details of a large inland sea and a vast desert in the Piedmont area led many to discount the veracity of his published writings. There is a North Carolina Highway Historical Marker north of Townsville, in Vance County.

Moses Ashley Curtis, Orange County

Like many others, Moses Ashley Curtis was drawn to North Carolina. Born in Massachusetts in 1808, he studied theology, tutored the children of Governor Edward Dudley, taught in Raleigh and finally became rector of the Protestant Episcopal Church in Hillsborough. Curtis frequently explored the mountains of Southern Appalachia, collecting for his own herbarium and working with other botanists like John Torrey, Asa Gray, Edward Tuckerman and Miles J. Berkeley. A.W. Chapman's 1860 work, *Flora of the Southern United States*, was dedicated to Curtis. Later in life, Curtis spent time retracing the steps of André Michaux and studying fungi. He published two books, and part of his herbaria is located at the University of North Carolina–Chapel Hill. Curtis died in 1872 and is buried at St. Matthew's Church, Hillsborough. There is a North Carolina Highway Historical Marker nearby.

MOUNTAINS

Hernando de Soto

Spanish conquistador Hernando de Soto was a world traveler who spent time exploring the West Indies as early as 1514. By 1530, he was one of the leading slave traders and richest men in Nicaragua. He continued to explore present-day Colombia and Peru, defeating the Incas. In 1538, De Soto set out with five to six hundred men to explore and conquer La Florida, looking for treasures like gold and silver along the way. They worked their way north, through Georgia and into the Carolinas. They moved through the Native American communities of Chalague (southwest of Charlotte), Guaquili (near Hickory) and Joara (northeast of Morganton). They crossed the Blue Ridge into present-day Avery County, forded the North Toe River and the French Broad and then moved on into Tennessee. While many of the Native Americans were friendly to the Spanish, De Soto treated them harshly. After four years, De Soto made his way to the Mississippi River, where he died of malaria. There were once several

Hernando de Soto led the first European expedition into what became North Carolina in the mid-sixteenth century. *Library of Congress.*

North Carolina Highway Historical Markers denoting various paths that De Soto and his men took while in North Carolina. They were located in the counties of Cherokee, Clay, Jackson and Macon but have since been removed based on recent research.

Juan Pardo, Fort San Juan, Burke County

In 1566, Domingo Fernandez and a group of Dominican priests sailed into Currituck Sound, claiming the area for Spain. That same year, Spanish explorer Juan Pardo left St. Helena Sound in South Carolina, heading toward western North Carolina. Eventually, Pardo and his men claimed the area for Spain, building six forts in the interior of North Carolina. The forts were short-lived, eventually falling to the Native Americans who lived in the area. A North Carolina Highway Historical Marker is in Morganton. There were once other markers in Macon, Clay and Cherokee Counties, but they were removed when the route was redefined.

Fort San Juan was established in present-day Burke County in 1567. *Author's collection.*

William Bartram

In the mid- to late 1700s came a new group of explorers. Instead of looking for new places to plant towns and settlers, these men came looking at the plants themselves, recording and collecting specimens of flora and fauna. The Bartram family looms large in that history, not just in North Carolina but also in the eastern United States. John Bartram is considered one of the great botanists in history. He traveled extensively collecting plants. His son, William Bartram Jr., settled in the Cape Fear River area in 1761, working at a store and exploring the area. After some personal misfortune, William set out to explore the South. He eventually described 358 species of plants, 130 of them new to science. There is a North Carolina Highway Historical Marker dedicated to Bartram in the Nantahala National Forest on the Macon-Swain County line, not far from where he met Atakullakulla in May 1776, and another near Ashwood, William Bartram's home in Bladen

County. There is also a Bartram Trail, more than eighty miles in length, that begins at Rabun Bald, near Highlands, and ends at Cheoah Bald. His observations were published in *Travels through North and South Carolina, Georgia, etc.* in 1791.

André Michaux, Lincoln County, Burke County, Avery County

André Michaux was so excited when he reached the top of Grandfather Mountain that he cried out, "Viva la France! Viva la United States!" Michaux thought he had reached the tallest mountain in the nation. Michaux was a French botanist and explorer who was sent to the United States to botanize the area for France in 1785. He named many plants, including the Carolina lily, rattlesnake fern, swamp thistle, umbrella leaf, water primrose, balsam ragwort, American aspen and the Catawba rhododendron. Michaux eventually made five trips to Western North Carolina, studying along the French Broad River, the Catawba River, the Linville River and the North Toe River. There are several North Carolina Highway Historical Markers commemorating his travels; these are found at the entrance of Grandfather Mountain and at Black Mountain, Morganton, Lincolnton and Bakersville. There is an exhibit on Michaux in the nature museum at Grandfather Mountain.

André Michaux was so excited when he climbed to the top of Grandfather Mountain that he sang the French national anthem. *Author's collection.*

Silas McDowell, Macon County

Born in South Carolina in 1795, Silas McDowell guided other botanists who visited the area, including John Lyon and Moses Curtis. His interests were widespread, including mineralogy, geology, zoology and Western North Carolina history. Living on a farm in Macon County, McDowell frequently wrote on the phenomenon of "thermal belts." There is a North Carolina Highway Historical Marker near Franklin commemorating his life, and he is buried at the Franklin Methodist Church Cemetery.

Asa Gray, Avery County, Ashe County

Asa Gray, the foremost nineteenth-century American botanist, took several trips through North Carolina. *Library of Congress.*

The vast wilderness of Southern Appalachia called many of the world's leading botanists to explore. Asa Gray, professor of botany at Harvard University, is considered the most important American botanist of the nineteenth century. Born in New York in 1810, he had earned a medical degree by the age of twenty-one. However, Gray was more interested in plants than medicine. He became friends with John Torrey and frequently corresponded with Charles Darwin. While studying Michaux's collection in Paris, Gray came upon an unidentified plant that he named Oconee bells. Michaux's notes simply stated that the plant was found high in the mountains of Western North Carolina. Gray set out in 1841 to find the plant, visiting Ashe County, Roan Mountain and Grandfather Mountain. Gray returned in 1843 but failed again to find the plant. Finally, in 1877, *Shortia galacifolia* was discovered—not in the High Country, but growing along the banks of the Catawba River near Marion. Gray visited North Carolina again in the spring of 1879. Traveling through Statesville, Gray explored McDowell County. There are North Carolina Highway Historical Markers at Grandfather Mountain, Jefferson and Bakersville commemorating his visits. There is also a Grandfather Mountain exhibit on the famed explorer.

Thomas Harbison, Macon County

Some of the botanists who came to explore the region had quite an impact. Thomas G. Harbison visited Western North Carolina while on a walking tour in the 1880s. The people of Highlands were so impressed that they asked him to return as a school principal, and he worked in Macon County schools from 1886 to 1896. From 1897 to 1903, Harbison worked for George W. Vanderbilt, collecting plants for the Biltmore Herbarium. He also collected in other states as well. His home, just outside Highlands, is included in the National Register of Historic Places, and there is a North Carolina Highway Historical Marker in Highlands.

Further Reading:
William Bartram, *The Travels of William Bartram* (2016)
A. Hunter Dupree, *Asa Gray: American Botanist, Friend of Darwin* (1988)
John Lawson, *A New Voyage to Carolina* (1709, 2014)

NORTH CAROLINA'S HISTORY OF CONSERVATION

Conservation in North Carolina goes back centuries. Early legislators enacted laws that protected waterways, certain game animals and tracts of timber as early as 1738. However, the early nineteenth-century demand for turpentine and late nineteenth-century demand for wood largely wrecked much of the forest across the state. Loss of habitat and overhunting led to a decline of native animals as well. Throughout the twentieth century, there was a gradual improvement of conditions throughout the state. There were laws that regulated the disposal of waste, prohibitions against the dumping of mining waste into creeks, the creation of the Fisheries Commission Board and the Department of Conservation and Development and the formation of the Stream Sanitation and Conservation Committee. The creation of the forestry school in the Biltmore Forest and the work of the Civilian Conservation Corps, "Roosevelt's Tree Army," took great leaps toward restoring parts of a wrecked ecosystem in the state.

COASTAL

Hofmann Forest, Onslow County

In 1934, the North Carolina Forestry Foundation purchased the seventy-nine-thousand-acre Hofmann Forest. The property was gifted to the North Carolina State Endowment Fund in 1977. Originally, the property was used to teach forestry practices to students at the North Carolina State University's College of Natural Resources. Today, the fifty-six thousand acres are used for timber and wood pulp production. There is a North Carolina Highway Historical Marker north of Jacksonville.

Mattamuskeet National Wildlife Refuge, New Holland, Hyde County

The old Mattamuskeet pumping station was turned into a hunting lodge by the Civilian Conservation Corps. *State Archives of North Carolina.*

A part of the Coastal North Carolina Wildlife Refuge Complex, the Mattamuskeet National Wildlife Refuge contains Lake Mattamuskeet, North Carolina's largest natural lake. The lake is just over forty thousand acres in size. There were attempts in the 1910s and 1920s to drain the area and turn it into viable farmland. Except for a brief period in the late 1920s, those attempts were unsuccessful. The property was sold to the federal government in 1934, and the Civilian Conservation Corps turned the old pumping station into a hunting lodge. The lodge closed in 1974. There are two North Carolina Highway Historical Markers that mention the area, both in Hyde County. There is a visitors' contact station near New Holland.

PIEDMONT

Thomas Gilbert Pearson, Guilford County

T. Gilbert Pearson, a self-taught taxidermist, traded his collection of mounted birds for two years of board and tuition at Guilford College in 1891. The trade tied a remarkable individual to North Carolina. Born in Indiana and growing up in Florida, Pearson was fascinated with birds. After graduating from college, he taught biology at Guilford College and then later at what is now University of North Carolina–Greensboro. Pearson organized the Audubon Society in North Carolina and helped push through a bill in 1903 establishing members of the Audubon Society as game wardens. He also became the first state game commissioner. He went on to serve as secretary and then president of the National Association of Audubon Societies. He died in 1943 and is buried at Green Hill Cemetery, Greensboro. A North Carolina Highway Historical Marker is in Greensboro.

Brown Creek Soil Conservation District, Anson County

The North Carolina General Assembly created the North Carolina Soil and Conservation District Law in 1937, allowing landowners to develop and implement soil conservation practices. The Brown Creek Soil Conservation District was created in Anson and Union Counties on August 3, 1937. The new district was the first such place in the United States. It included the home of Hugh Hammon Bennett, considered the father of the soil and water conservation movement in the United States. A North Carolina Highway Historical Marker about the district is located east of Polkton, and another marker to Bennett is located west of Wadesboro.

MOUNTAINS

Cradle of Forestry, Pisgah Forest, Transylvania County

It is not possible to overstate the importance of the forestry school established in Western North Carolina. Businessman George W. Vanderbilt II acquired tens of thousands of acres in the region in the late nineteenth century. On part of this property, he built the Biltmore house. Many of his other vast properties were logged. Trees were not replanted, leading to topsoil erosion, silting of streams and frequent fires. On a trip to Europe, Vanderbilt observed forests that were reclaimed through management. Vanderbilt hired Gifford Pinchot to develop a plan for the property and then hired Dr. Carl Schenck, who went beyond the 125,000 acres that Vanderbilt owned. He started the Biltmore Forest School. The school operated for eleven years, pioneering creative forestry management and conservation. The core of the site is known today as the Cradle of

The schoolhouse for training foresters is one of the original structures from the Biltmore Forestry School, now the Cradle of Forestry in America Heritage Site, Jackson County. *Library of Congress.*

Forestry, an American Heritage Site. There are hiking trails, restored buildings and a Climax steam locomotive. Inside the Forest Discovery Center is a twenty-six-minute documentary, a hands-on exhibit, a café and a gift shop.

Further Reading:

Oliver H. Orr Jr., *Saving American Birds: T. Gilbert Pearson and the Founding of the Audubon Movement* (1992)

BLOOMS OF THE PAST

HISTORIC GARDENS

North Carolina is covered with a rich bounty of plant life. The state's diverse ecosystems host plants as various as the landscapes where they grow, from the marine live oaks of the coast, inland marshes and grass-sedge bogs to the majestic hardwoods and dense mountain laurel of the Southern Appalachians. A great way to explore both native and imported plants and trees is to visit one of the many public gardens across the state that celebrates natural history while also serving as a historic landmark.

PIEDMONT

Daniel Stowe Botanical Gardens, Gaston County

Daniel J. Stowe had an interest in a wide variety of subjects He was a benefactor of the Gaston Museum of Art and History, collected antiques and traveled the world. A cofounder of a textile company, he also left the enduring legacy of the Daniel Stowe Botanical Gardens. Located on 380 acres, the garden opened in October 1999. The Visitor Pavilion has eight rooms and twelve fountains. The Gardens also include the Orchid Conservatory, the only facility of that type in the area, and Lost Hollow: The Kimbrell Children's Garden, which opened in 2014. The Piedmont Prairie Garden opened in 2019, providing visitors with a look at the type of ecosystem that once blanketed the area.

Old Salem Museums and Gardens, Forsyth County

Old Salem was founded in 1766 by Moravian settlers. The Moravians were Christians from the modern-day Czech Republic. They migrated to colonial America in search of economic opportunities and the chance to spread their beliefs. Gardening was fundamental to their lifestyle, and several botanists called the community home. The largest garden is the Single Brothers Garden, where trees, flowers and vegetables are grown. The Miksch Garden is a seed-to-table garden used in interpretive programs at the site. The Triebel Garden is also a kitchen garden. All of the gardens at Old Salem are tied to the history of the area and the Moravians.

North Carolina Botanical Garden, Orange County

Conserving our natural landscapes is one of the leading themes of the North Carolina Botanical Garden on the campus of the University of North Carolina–Chapel Hill. The garden had its origins in 1903, when William Coker, professor of botany, began planting a collection of trees and shrubs. This became known as the Coker Arboretum. The garden system on campus grew over time. In 1952, 70 acres of forested land were dedicated to garden development. Another 103 acres were added by horticulturist William Lanier Hunt. Nature trails opened to the public in 1966. There are eight major collections at the site, showcasing plant life from the Mountains, Sandhills and Coastal Plains.

Reynolda Gardens of Wake Forest University, Forsyth County

Reynolda was once the home of tobacco tycoon R.J. Reynolds and his wife, Katharine Smith Reynolds. As with any good country estate, formal gardens were a requirement at Reynolda. The gardens contain not only the four-acre formal plot but also woodlands and wetlands, as well as a 1913 greenhouse. The Reynolda Garden property was donated to Wake Forest University by Mary Reynolds Babcock, daughter of R.J. Reynolds. In 1995, the gardens were returned to their original design.

Sarah P. Duke Gardens, Durham County

Begun in 1934 as a garden for irises, the garden was created as a memorial to Sarah P. Duke, the wife of Benjamin N. Duke, one of the benefactors of Duke University. The gardens opened to the public in 1939. The original gardens were designed by Ellen Biddle Shipman, who designed around 650 other gardens. Visitors can find gardens of roses, native plants of the southeastern United States and the W.L. Culberson Asiatic Arboretum, along with five miles of walking trails.

MOUNTAINS

Daniel Boone Native Gardens, Watauga County

Daniel Boone found an incredibly varied biosphere when he was hunting throughout northwestern North Carolina in the 1760s. In the mid-twentieth century, the garden club in Boone began working on developing native gardens to allow modern visitors easy access to many of the remarkable plants Boone found when he traveled to the region so long ago. In 1963, the Daniel Boone Native Gardens opened. The site features a wishing

Dating to the early 1800s, the Squire Boone cabin in the Daniel Boone Native Gardens pays homage to the early Yadkin River pioneer. *Author's collection.*

well, a reflecting pool and an original cabin, alongside thriving specimens of numerous local plants, like jack-in-the-pulpit, skunk cabbage, shooting star, cinnamon fern, cone flower, spiderwort and ironweed. The gardens are located next to the Hickory Ridge Homestead.

North Carolina Arboretum, Buncombe County

Located close to the Blue Ridge Parkway, the North Carolina Arboretum was established by the University of North Carolina System in 1986. The park is 434 acres and contains hiking and biking trails, along with plenty of opportunities for children to connect with nature. There are pollinator gardens, native wildflowers and a Bonsai Exhibition Garden. Frederick Law Olmsted played a role in the foundation of the garden. He was working on the designs for the gardens at nearby Biltmore Estate and had the idea of creating a large research arboretum on the estate. While it took many years to implement his vision, Olmsted is honored today with a North Carolina Arboretum statue commemorating him as the father of American landscape architecture.

Further Reading:

Peter Loewer, *Gardens of North Carolina: A Traveler's Guide* (2007)
B.W. Wells, *The Natural Gardens of North Carolina* (1967)

FARMS, MANSIONS AND HOMES

HISTORIC HOUSES OF NORTH CAROLINA

There are many historic structures in North Carolina. The oldest residence documented by dendrochronology is the Lane House in Edenton. Privately owned, the house dates to 1718–19. Located in the town of Bath, St. Thomas Episcopal Church is the oldest surviving church in North Carolina. The church was constructed in 1734. St. Paul's Episcopal Church in Edenton was constructed in 1736. The houses described here are all open to the public.

COASTAL

Cupola House, Chowan County

Constructed in Edenton in 1756–58, the two-story Cupola House is one of only two period houses in the American South built with a "jutt," or overhanging second floor. It is also considered the finest wooden example of the Jacobean style of architecture in the South. In 1918, local citizens purchased and restored the home, opening it to visitors.

James Iredell House, Chowan County

Born in 1751, James Iredell was an important leader in colonial and early republic history. His essay "To the Inhabitants of Great Britain" argued

The Cupola House, constructed in 1756–58, is the second-oldest house in Edenton. *Library of Congress.*

against parliamentary supremacy over the American colonies. Iredell served as a state judge and attorney general, and in 1780, he was nominated by George Washington as an associate justice of the U.S. Supreme Court. The original portion of the house was built in 1800—a two-story, L-shaped frame dwelling with Georgian- and Federalist-style elements. The house is now a part of Historic Edenton, a state historic site.

Newbold-White House, Perquimans County

The oldest North Carolina house that is now open to the public is the 1730 brick home on the Perquimans River, built by Abraham and Judith Sanders. The home, located in Hertford, has been restored by the Perquimans County Restoration Association. Usually tied up nearby is the *Periauger*, a reproduction colonial boat.

Palmer-March House, Beaufort County

Built in 1744, the Palmer-Marsh House is a well-preserved example of a large colonial town house. The building was constructed for Michael Coutanch, who used some of the ground-floor rooms as a store. When the colonial legislature met in Bath, the body used this structure. The house was given to the state in 1963, and it is now a state historic site.

Somerset Place, Washington County

Originally, Somerset Place was composed of 100,000 acres near Creswell. The double-piazza house was constructed by Josiah Collins III in 1838–39. The property once contained fifty different structures, such as slave cabins, barns, a sawmill, a gristmill and stables. In the 1930s, parts of the property were included as part of Pettigrew State Park. The property is now a state historic site.

Tryon Palace, Craven County

Built between 1767 and 1770 in New Bern, Tryon Palace was the home of the royal governor of North Carolina and his family. It was also the capital of the state. During the American Revolution, Patriot forces took over the building, and the first sessions of the General Assembly met there. Tryon Palace was home to North Carolina's first four governors following statehood. The capital was moved to Raleigh in 1794. A fire in 1798 destroyed much of the original structure, with only the stable office remaining. The building was rebuilt in the 1950s and is now a North Carolina State Historic site with re-created historic gardens.

Tryon Palace was the official residence of royal governors between 1770 and 1775 and for several state governors after North Carolina declared statehood in 1776. *State Archives of North Carolina.*

PIEDMONT

Governor's Mansion, Wake County

Construction began on a new governor's mansion in Raleigh in 1883 and was completed in 1891. The building was designed by architects Samuel Sloan and A.G. Bauer. President Franklin D. Roosevelt once described the house, constructed in the Queen Anne style, as the "most beautiful governor's residence interior in America." The house was placed in the National Register of Historic Places in 1970.

Mordecai House, Wake County

In 1785, Joel Lane began working on a new home in Raleigh for his son, Henry. The property passed to Moses Mordecai, and the house was transformed by a Greek Revival addition. The property was purchased by the City of Raleigh in 1967, and the Mordecai Historical Park was created. The park contains not only the Mordecai House but also a barn, a plantation office, a kitchen, a law office, a chapel and the Andrew Johnson Birthplace.

Alexander Rock House, Mecklenburg County

Hezekiah Alexander moved his family from Pennsylvania to North Carolina in about 1768. By 1774, they had finished a stone house in Mecklenburg County. The home, which is about five thousand square feet, is composed of local stones, the walls of which are two feet thick in places. Alexander was a member of Mecklenburg's Committee of Safety, composed the Mecklenburg Resolves and participated in drafting North Carolina's first constitution. In 1943, the house was donated to become a museum, and it is currently owned by the Charlotte Museum of History.

Blandwood Mansion, Guilford County

Construction on Blandwood Mansion began in 1795. It was a simple, four-room, Federal-style farmhouse. Its transformation into an Italian villa began with Governor John M. Morehead, who lived in the house from

The first North Carolina governor to occupy the new Governor's Mansion was David Fowle in January 1891. *State Archives of North Carolina.*

Blandwood Mansion in Greensboro was the home of Governor John M. Morehead. *State Archives of North Carolina.*

1827 to 1866. The house is considered the most important building in Greensboro and its oldest. Preservation Greensboro Inc. has owned the house since 1966.

Duke Homestead, Durham County

Washington Duke is one of the truly foundational people in North Carolina history. In 1852, he moved his family into a new house, known today as the Duke Homestead. Duke was already growing tobacco prior to the Civil War, but following the war, he began to manufacture pipe tobacco. His business soon grew into the largest tobacco manufacturing enterprise in the world. The family moved to Durham in 1874. The homestead, with the accompanying Tobacco Museum, is now a state historic site.

Heck-Andrews House, Wake County

Raleigh's best example of a Second Empire–style house is the Heck-Andrews House, completed circa 1870. It was the first large-scale home constructed in Raleigh following the Civil War. The home was owned by the Heck family until 1916, when the Andrews family purchased it. The State of North Carolina purchased the home in 1987 and restored the exterior before selling it to the North Carolina Association of Realtors in 2016.

Reynolda House, Forsyth County

An excellent example of the American Country House Movement is the 1917 Reynolda House. The thirty-four-thousand-square foot, sixty-four-room home was constructed for Katharine Smith and R.J. Reynolds, the founder of the Reynolds Tobacco Company. The home now contains an American art museum and extensive gardens.

Richmond Hill, Yadkin County

North Carolina chief justice Richmond M. Pearson was one of the most influential men of the nineteenth century. He operated a law school that

Duke Homestead, now a state historic site, was the home of tobacco pioneer Washington M. Duke. *Author's collection.*

Chief Justice Richmond M. Pearson operated his law school from the grounds of his home, Richmond Hill. *Author's collection.*

educated fellow jurists, congressmen, governors and newspaper editors from his home near East Bend in Yadkin County. While the cabins that housed the school and students no longer stand, the Pearson home has been restored and is open to the public certain weekends every year.

Rosedale, Mecklenburg County

Constructed in 1805 by Archibald Frew and at times known as "Frew's Folly," Rosedale is a beautiful example of a Federalist-style home. After Frew died in 1823, the home passed to his brother-in-law, state senator William Davidson. It stayed in the family until the 1980s, when it was acquired by the Historic Preservation Society of North Carolina. The home was restored, and in 1993, Historic Rosedale was opened to the public.

Stagville, Durham County

Stagville was the home of the Bennehan and Cameron families from the 1770s to 1865. Composed of roughly thirty thousand acres, it was one of the largest plantations in North Carolina. While the family held nine hundred enslaved people at one time, the house is somewhat modest in comparison to other large plantations in the Deep South. Still surviving are four two-story slave dwellings. Historic Stagville State Historic Site has been operated by the State of North Carolina since 1978.

MOUNTAINS

Biltmore, Buncombe County

Built between 1889 and 1895 for George Washington Vanderbilt II, Biltmore is the largest privately owned house in the United States. The four-acre house has 250 rooms, including 35 bedrooms, 43 bathrooms, 65 fireplaces and 3 kitchens. The house has hosted U.S. Presidents William McKinley, Theodore Roosevelt, Jimmy Carter, Ronald Reagan and Barack Obama. Biltmore is considered one of the most prominent examples of Gilded Age architecture in the world and is open for a variety of tour experiences. Special exhibits are often on display at the house or one of the other facilities on the property.

Biltmore, near Asheville, is the largest private residence in the United States. This image dates from April 29, 1924. *Library of Congress.*

Carson House, McDowell County

Constructed in 1793 by Colonel John Carson, the enormous three-story Carson House served as a stop for many weary travelers. David Crockett, Sam Houston and Andrew Jackson all stayed at the home. The house passed through several owners over the years, and in 1964, it was purchased by concerned citizens and opened as a museum.

Cone Manor House, Watauga County

Many wealthy nineteenth- and twentieth-century businessmen built summer homes in the mountains. Moses H. Cone was a textile entrepreneur, conservationist and philanthropist. He and his wife, the son and daughter of German and Jewish immigrants, constructed Flat Top Manor in the late 1890s. The home contained twenty-three rooms, while the grounds included two lakes, apple orchards and twenty-five miles of carriage roads. The property passed to the National Park Service in the late 1940s. The main level of the house is open as a craft center, and tours of the upper floors are sometimes offered.

Fort Defiance, Caldwell County

Constructed by Revolutionary War veteran William Lenoir in 1792, Fort Defiance has been restored and features more than three hundred pieces of original furnishings. Lenoir and other members of the family are buried in a cemetery on the grounds. The county of Lenoir and the town of Lenoir are both named after the general. Tours are available, and special events are often hosted at the site.

Smith-McDowell House, Buncombe County

James Smith, rumored to be the first child of European parents born west of the Blue Ridge, began construction on a brick house in the 1840s. The home was purchased in 1857 by William McDowell. The house was converted into a school in 1951. Later, the house, located in Asheville, was restored and opened as a museum in 1981.

McElroy House, Yancey County

John W. McElroy was an up-and-coming businessman of Western North Carolina in the 1840s. Yancey County had just been carved out of Buncombe County, and McElroy was serving as clerk of Superior Court while dealing

The circa 1840 McElroy House in Burnsville is rumored to have been used as a hospital during an April 1864 skirmish. *Author's collection.*

in real estate. He had a large timber-frame home constructed, overlooking the town square in Burnsville. By the time of the Civil War, McElroy had sold the house. It was reportedly used as a hospital during a raid in April 1864 and then was owned by a Union veteran. The house is now a part of the Rush Wray Museum of Yancey County History.

Further Reading:
Catherine W. Bishier, *North Carolina Architecture* (1990)

LOCKED UP IN THE PAST

HISTORIC JAILS

Old jails might not top the list of places to visit for some people, but many of these sites showcase vast amounts of history. Several former jails across North Carolina have been turned into some of the best local museums in the state.

COASTAL

Chowan County Jail, Chowan County

Edenton's founding dates back to 1712. There were several jails in the community prior to the construction of the 1825 Chowan County Jail. The brick walls on the ground level are an astonishing twenty-nine inches thick. The jail was used to house twenty-one African Americans arrested during the Nat Turner Rebellion in 1831. They were suspected of conspiracy, but the first to be tried was found innocent, so the judge released all of the others. This facility closed in 1975—the longest-serving jail not only in North Carolina but also in the entire United States. It was finally reopened as a museum in 2018.

Old Brunswick Jail, Brunswick County

After losing an earlier jail to arson, Brunswick County opened what is now the Old Brunswick Jail in 1904. It was closed in 1971 and, in 1984, became a museum operated by the Southport Historical Society. The most famous "prisoner" at the jail was Sissy Spacek, who went behind bars here to film the movie *Crimes of the Heart* in 1986.

Camden County Jail, Camden County

Located beside the historic courthouse in Camden, the old Camden County Jail was constructed in 1910. Built in the Colonial Revival style, the structure features an iron cellblock, or bullpen, on the second floor. The Camden County Heritage Museum and Historic Jail opened in September 2017. There are numerous displays throughout the museum, featuring local personalities, military events and the greater Albemarle area.

PIEDMONT

Halifax Jail, Halifax County

The little community of Halifax is rich in history. It was founded in the 1760s as a port town and played a role during the American Revolution. Halifax has many historic buildings, including an 1838 jail. Two other jails sat near this spot in the past. Both were set on fire by inmates in escape attempts.

The Halifax County Jail was built in 1838. *State Archives of North Carolina.*

Old Jail Museum, Alexander County

Like many of the old jails in North Carolina, the Alexander County Jail, constructed in 1913, housed not only prisoners but the jailer and his family as well. Today, the Old Jail serves as the Alexander County Ancestry Association's Genealogical Research Library.

Granville County Jail, Granville County

Constructed around 1850, the Granville County Jail was slated for demolition when the Oxford Woman's Club stepped in and leased the building for a museum. That lease was transferred to the Granville County Historical Society in 1994, and the new museum opened in 1996. Today, it is known as the Granville History Museum and Harris Exhibit Hall.

MOUNTAINS

Avery County Historical Museum, Avery County

Constructed in 1913, the Avery County Jail sits beside the courthouse in Newland. Avery County was the last North Carolina county created. The jail was used until 1970, and in 1976, it was opened as the Avery County

The Avery County Jail was in service from 1913 to 1970 and has been a museum since 1976. *Author's collection.*

Historical Museum. There are displays on local history throughout, with rooms dedicated to the military, local stores and schools. The original pens, or cells, are still in place on the second story of the building. The first floor was for housing the family of the jail keeper. Behind the jail is the Linville Depot and the ET&WNC Caboose 505.

Old Wilkes Jail, Wilkes County

Built in 1859, the Wilkes County Jail served to incarcerate prisoners until 1915. It was saved from demolition and opened to the public in the 1970s. Like other early jails, this one housed both inmates and the jailer's family as well. Among the famous prisoners here were Otto Wood, known for breaking out of ten other jails (but not this one), and Tom Dula, who was hanged for the murder of Laura Foster. The restored building is a part of the Wilkes Heritage Museum.

Clay County Jail, Clay County

The old Clay County Jail was opened in 1912. It originally lacked electricity and perhaps lacked plumbing for the inmates and the family who lived there. In 1972, the old jail was closed as the new jail opened. Two years later, the building was turned over to the Clay County Historical and Arts Council for a museum. There are exhibits on local medical professionals, education and African American heritage, as well as a quilting room, along with the cells themselves.

Further Reading:

Michael C. Hardy and Jimmie Daniels, *Families, Friends, and Felons: Growing Up in the Avery County Jail* (2008)

REMEMBER ME

HISTORIC CEMETERIES

Anyone who wants to understand the history of a town or community should always go visit the local cemetery as a first step. There, carved in stone, are the hopes, dreams and accomplishments of the people who lived nearby. Sometimes an epitaph tells a fairly complete story, while at other times the stone itself tells the visitor a little bit of history. A broken column often symbolizes a life cut short, crossed swords speak of military service and a Masonic or Odd Fellows emblem denotes a fraternal brotherhood. There are thousands of cemeteries across the Old North State with stories just waiting to be explored. Some are must-visit historic destinations that both preserve the past and tell its stories.

COASTAL

British Cemetery, Hyde County

In May 1942, the HMT *Bedfordshire* was patrolling the coastal area of North Carolina when the ship was torpedoed by a German submarine. All thirty-seven members of the crew were lost. The bodies of four British sailors washed ashore near Ocracoke. Two were identified, and two were unknown. They were buried at the local cemetery. Today, the burial site has been leased to the British government. A British flag flies over the graves, and a joint American-British memorial service is held every year. There is another British cemetery located on Hatteras Island containing the graves of two British sailors who likewise washed ashore during World War II.

Calvary Episcopal Church Cemetery, Edgecombe County

The history of the Episcopal Church goes back centuries. What became Tarboro's Calvary Episcopal Church began as an Anglican body. After the American Revolution, the church was reborn as an Episcopal church. The cemetery is much older than the current building, which is Gothic in style and was consecrated in 1868. Among notable burials are Henry Toole Clark, governor from 1861 to 1862; William Dorsey Pender, a Confederate general mortally wounded at Gettysburg; and Colonel John Thomas Mercer, who was killed in the fighting at Plymouth in April 1864.

In 1923, a group of citizens gathered to dedicate the grave marker for William Dorsey Pender, mortally wounded during the Battle of Gettysburg. *North Carolina Museum of History.*

Colonial Churchyard, Halifax County

As the name implies, the Colonial Churchyard in Halifax stretches back before the American Revolution. A few of the graves are enclosed in grave houses and box tombs. Among those interred here are John Cooper Sr. (1730–1794), member of the Second Provincial Congress; John Sitgreaves (1757–1802), Continental Congressman and judge; Sarah Jones Davie (1762–1802), wife of Governor William R. Davie; Abraham Hodge (1759–1805), early newspaper editor; and Junius Daniel (1828–1864), Confederate general killed in Virginia.

St. Paul's Episcopal Church, Chowan County

For several years, Edenton served as the capital of North Carolina. The history of St. Paul's Episcopal Church Cemetery stretches back to 1722. Among the more than seven hundred graves here are those of three North Carolina colonial governors: Thomas Pollock (1654–1722), Charles Eden (1673–1722) and Gabriel Johnston (1698–1752). All three graves were moved to this location.

Oakdale Cemetery, New Hanover

Since the first burial in February 1855, Oakdale Cemetery in Wilmington has expanded to become one of the largest cemeteries in the state. It is also a classic southern cemetery, with interesting monuments and moss-covered oak trees. Among the notable burials are Henry Bacon (1866–1924), an architect best remembered for designing the Lincoln Memorial in Washington, D.C.; David Brinkley (1920–2003), television newscaster; Edward B. Dudley (1789–1855), governor, U.S. congressman and railroad president; George Davis (1820–1896), Confederate senator and attorney general; William H.C. Whiting (1824–1865), Confederate major general; Rose O'Neal Greenhow (1814–1864), Confederate spy; and Mary Lily Kenan Flagler Bingham (1867–1917), who, upon the death of her first husband, Henry Flagler, became the richest woman in the country. The cemetery also contains the grave of Nancy Martin, buried sitting in a chair inside a rum barrel after she had died at sea; a Confederate section, with more than three hundred soldiers; a section for victims of the yellow fever epidemic in the 1860s; a Jewish section; and a section for members of the Odd Fellows.

St. Paul's Episcopal Church Cemetery, in Edenton, has more than seven hundred graves, including those of three governors. *State Archives of North Carolina.*

Old Burying Ground, Carteret County

Quite possibly the most iconic cemetery in North Carolina is the Old Burying Ground in Beaufort. The cemetery was established in the early 1700s and was deeded to the town in 1731. Among the interesting and historic graves here are those of another girl who was buried in a barrel of rum when she died at sea, as well as Otway Burns (1775–1850), North Carolina's greatest naval hero of the War of 1812. Burns, a privateer, is buried under one of the cannons from his ship, the *Snap Dragon*. A British officer who died in the 1700s and several Confederate and Union soldiers are buried here as well.

The Old Burying Ground in Beaufort has many interesting graves, including that of Otway Burns, War of 1812 privateer. *Author's collection.*

New Bern National Cemetery, Craven County

Established on February 1, 1867, the New Bern National Cemetery received the remains of Federal soldiers who were killed in the Battle of New Bern, as well as those who were killed or died of disease in the surrounding areas during the Civil War, including Beaufort and Hatteras. There are monuments from New Jersey, Massachusetts, Connecticut and Rhode Island in the cemetery, which was listed in the National Register of Historic Places in 1997.

Wilmington National Cemetery, New Hanover County

The national cemetery in Wilmington was established in 1867. It is the final resting place for Federal soldiers killed at the 1865 battle of Fort Fisher, including a number of African American soldiers. The cemetery was used for a number of years after the war, but it is now closed to new interments.

Willow Dale Cemetery, Wayne County

Located just a few blocks from downtown Goldsboro, Willow Dale Cemetery was designed in 1853 by Charles Nelson. The site has a mass grave of eight hundred Confederate soldiers, along with a Jewish section that contains the grave of women's rights activist Gertrude Weil (1879–1971). Other noteworthy interments include Clyde King (1924–2010), major-league baseball player, manager and coach; Curtis H. Brooks (1816–1901), governor and U.S. congressman; William G. Lewis (1835–1901), Confederate general; and Kenneth C. Royal (1894–1971), secretary of war under President Harry S Truman and brigadier general during World War II.

PIEDMONT

Cross Creek Cemetery, Cumberland County

Established in 1785, Cross Creek Cemetery has more than 1,170 graves and is the oldest cemetery in Fayetteville. Among those interred here are James C. Dobbin (1814–1857), congressman and secretary of the navy; Warren Winslow (1810–1862), congressman and governor; Charles Manly Stedman (1841–1930), lieutenant governor and congressman—the last Confederate veteran to hold that position; and Elliott Daingerfield (1859–1932), one of North Carolina's most prolific artists. There is a Confederate section in Cross Creek where soldiers who died locally during the war are interred, as well as Brookside, an area dedicated to burials for African Americans. Interred in the Brookside section is Ezekiel Smith (1852–1922), U.S. minister to Liberia.

Elmwood Cemetery, Mecklenburg County

At seventy-plus acres in Charlotte, Elmwood Cemetery is actually three cemeteries: Elmwood, Potter's Field and Pinewood. Elmwood was first opened in 1853. Potter's Field was the place of burial for people who could not afford to buy a plot. Pinewood was beyond the Potter's Field and contained the graves of African Americans. Notable graves include those of Rufus Barringer (1821–1895), Confederate general; Cameron A. Morrison

(1869–1953), governor, congressman and U.S. senator; William H. Bobbitt (1900–1992), judge and chief justice of the North Carolina Supreme Court; Oscar S. Heizer (1869–1956), U.S. consul in Constantinople, Trebizond, Baghdad, Jerusalem and Algiers; Randolph Scott (1898–1987), World War I veteran and actor; Annie Lowrie Alexander (1864–1929), the first licensed female physician in the South; and Julia McGehee Alexander (1876–1957), the second woman to practice law in North Carolina and first to serve in the North Carolina House. Within the cemetery are the Fireman's Memorial (1883) and a Confederate section containing 175 graves along with several monuments. In Pinewood is the grave of W.W. Smith (1862–1937), Charlotte's first noted Black architect.

Joppa Cemetery, Davie County

The Joppa Cemetery is not a large cemetery, but it is significant. Lying on the outskirts of Mocksville, the cemetery contains around 450 graves. Originally called Burying Ground Ridge, the cemetery contains the grave of Squire and Sarah (Morgan) Boone, the parents of Daniel Boone. They came from Pennsylvania via Virginia, settling in the Yadkin River Valley area in late 1751. A North Carolina Highway Historical Marker marks the cemetery.

A small graveyard just outside Mocksville, the Joppa Cemetery contains the graves of the parents of Daniel Boone. *Author's collection.*

Oakwood Cemetery, Wake County

Raleigh's Oakwood Cemetery could easily be considered the official cemetery for North Carolina. Created in 1869, the cemetery includes more than twenty-two thousand graves. These include seven governors, five U.S. senators, eight North Carolina chief justices of the Supreme Court, four Confederate generals and two secretaries of the U.S. Navy. Jim Valvano (1946–1993), North Carolina State University basketball coach, and Berrien Upshaw (1901–1949), husband of Margaret Mitchell, are also interred here. There is a large Confederate section containing the graves of those originally buried at the Rock Quarry Cemetery and those from North Carolina who fell at Gettysburg. The famed "Boy Colonel" of the Confederacy, Henry King Burgwyn Jr., killed while leading the Twenty-Sixth North Carolina Gettysburg, is also interred at Oakwood. Others buried here include Cornelia Petty Jerman (1874–1946), noted suffragist; Carle A. Woodruff (1841–1913), Medal of Honor winner; and Leonidas L. Polk (1837–1892), journalist and founder of the Populist Party.

Old City Cemetery, Wake County

For such a small cemetery—only four acres—the old City Cemetery in Raleigh has a large number of graves of people important to North Carolina history. The cemetery was created in 1798 with sections for residents, visitors and African Americans. Anna J. Cooper (1858–1964), an

The Old City Cemetery in Raleigh seems small, but within its gates are the graves of several prominent North Carolinians. *State Archives of North Carolina.*

author, activist and one of the most prominent African American scholars in United States history, is buried at the City Cemetery, as are Lawrence O. Branch (1820–1862), railroad president, U.S. congressman and Confederate general who was killed in action at Antietam; Charles Manley (1795–1871), governor; and Joel Lane (1740–1795), judge and delegate to the North Carolina Constitutional Convention, who is considered the "Father of Raleigh."

Old English Cemetery, Rowan County

In December 1775, Daniel Little died and was buried at what is now the Old English Cemetery in Salisbury. He was probably the first. The surprising name "English Cemetery" can be attributed to a rumor that buried in this cemetery are British soldiers who died in 1781 when the British army occupied Salisbury. Notable graves include those of John W. Ellis (1820–1861), governor, and Francis Burton Craige (1811–1875), U.S. congressman and member of the Confederate Provisional Congress.

Old First Presbyterian Church, Guilford County

Now nestled in between the Greensboro Historical Museum and the local library, the First Presbyterian Church Cemetery has a storied past. The church was organized in 1824, and the first recorded burial in the cemetery was in 1831. Among the notables here are John Motley Morehead (1796–1866), governor of North Carolina and representative in the Confederate Provisional Congress, and John A. Gilmer (1805–1868), who represented his section of the state in both the U.S. and Confederate Congresses. The Presbyterian church now houses the Greensboro History Museum.

Old Settlers' Cemetery, Mecklenburg County

Located in the heart of Uptown Charlotte, the Old Settlers' Cemetery is the oldest cemetery in the city. The first grave dates to 1776. Among the notable burials here are Thomas Polk (circa 1732–1794), Continental officer and member of the North Carolina House, North Carolina

Provincial Congress and Council of State and great-uncle of president James K. Polk; George Graham (1758–1826), a militia major general who fought at the "Battle of the Hornets"; and Nathaniel Alexander (1756–1808), governor and U.S. congressman.

Hillsborough Old Town Cemetery, Orange County

Established in 1757, the Old Town Cemetery in Hillsborough was once the final resting place of William Hooper, one of North Carolina's signers of the Declaration of Independence. Hooper was moved to the Guilford Court House National Military Park in 1894. Still buried at Old Town Cemetery is William A. Graham (1804–1875), U.S. senator, governor, secretary of the navy, vice presidential candidate and Confederate senator.

Salem Cemetery, Forsyth County

Adjoining the Moravian cemeteries in Winston-Salem is the Salem Cemetery. Charted in 1857, the cemetery has numerous notables interred within its boundaries. These include William R. Boggs (1829–1911), Confederate general and university professor; Robert B. Glenn (1857–1920), governor; Thomas H. Davis (1918–1999), founder of Piedmont Airlines; and Richard J. Reynolds (1850–1918), founder of R.J. Reynolds Tobacco Company.

Salisbury National Cemetery, Salisbury

Salisbury was one of the many locations used as a prison during the Civil War. The prison housed not only Federal prisoners but also civilians and political dissidents. Over the course of war, just over five thousand Federal soldiers died and were interred at what became the Salisbury National Cemetery. Other Federal soldiers who died in places like Charlotte were moved to the cemetery after the war ended. The cemetery continues to operate to this day, with more than twenty-six thousand burials as of 2021.

Raleigh National Cemetery, Raleigh

During the Civil War, there were numerous hospitals established across the state. One of those complexes was located in Raleigh. Men, both Confederate and Union, who died at the hospital were buried at the Rock Quarry Cemetery. After the war, the Federals forced local residents to disinter their dead, and the cemetery became the Raleigh National Cemetery. Federal soldiers killed at Averasboro, Smithfield, Bentonville and Goldsboro were reinterred in Raleigh. The cemetery has six thousand interments, many post–Civil War, and is closed to further interments.

WESTERN

St. John in the Wilderness Cemetery, Henderson County

There are few more picturesque cemeteries in North Carolina than the one that surrounds St. John in the Wilderness Episcopal Church. The church had its beginnings in 1834 as a private family chapel. In 1836, the property was given to the Episcopal diocese. The church was largely used by families from the Lowcountry of South Carolina who visited the area during the summer months. The cemetery also contains a section for the enslaved. Among the notables buried at St. John are Lewis W. Haskell (1868–1938), U.S. consul in Salina Cruz, Hull, Belgrade, Geneva, Algiers and Zurich; Christopher G. Memminger (1803–1888), member of the Confederate Provisional Congress and Confederate secretary of the treasury; Campbell King (1871–1953), a general during World War I; Frank L. FitzSimons Sr. (1897–1980), author of the three-volume *From the Banks of the Oklawaha*; and Edward P. King Jr. (1884–1958), a World War II general who was forced to surrender the Philippines in 1942.

Riverside Cemetery, Buncombe County

Founded in 1885, Riverside Cemetery, like most Victorian cemeteries, was designed to be both a burial ground and a public park. The cemetery contains more than fourteen thousand graves, including the graves of eighteen German sailors from World War I, prisoners of war who died in a local hospital. Literary stars Thomas Wolfe (1900–1938) and O. Henry

(1862–1910) are buried here under modest stones. Politicians buried here include Zebulon Baird Vance (1830–1894), governor and U.S. senator; Jeter C. Pritchard (1857–1921), U.S. senator and judge; Richmond Pearson (1852–1923), congressman and U.S. minister to Persia, Greece and Montenegro; Thomas L. Clingman (1812–1897), U.S. senator and Confederate general; Locke Craig (1860–1924), governor; Robert B. Vance (1828–1899), Confederate general and U.S. congressman; and Allen T. Davidson (1819–1905), Confederate congressman. George "Buck" Redfern (1902–1964), major-league baseball player; Lamar Stringfield (1897–1959), composer; and George Masa (1881–1933), photographer, are also interred at Riverside.

Further Reading:

Henry King, *Tar Heel Tombstones and the Tales They Tell* (1990)

Ruth Little, *Sticks and Stones: Three Centuries of North Carolina Gravemarkers* (1998)

PRESIDENTS, VICE PRESIDENTS, ALSO-RANS AND A FIRST LADY

PRESIDENTS

Many presidents of the United States have visited North Carolina at some point, and modern presidential contenders often campaign heavily in the state. Some of the early presidents visited only once or twice. George Washington, in 1791, took a tour of the southern states, visiting sites including Halifax, Tarboro, Greenville, New Bern and Wilmington on his way south and Charlotte, Salisbury and Salem on his return trip north. James Madison made a southern tour in 1819, visiting Edenton, New Bern and Wilmington. James Buchanan visited Raleigh and Chapel Hill in June 1859. Theodore Roosevelt visited Raleigh in October 1905. His cousin, Franklin D. Roosevelt, visited in September 1940, speaking at the dedication of the Great Smoky Mountains National Park. Harry Truman was in Raleigh and New Bern in 1948. John F. Kennedy visited Chapel Hill in 1961. U.S. Grant and Woodrow Wilson both visited the state prior to becoming president. Wilson actually lived in Wilmington from 1874 to 1882. There are some presidents, vice presidents, candidates and one first lady who had even deeper ties to the Tar Heel State than a visit or a temporary stay.

Sculpted by Charles Keck, the monument depicting the three presidents with North Carolina ties was dedicated on the grounds of the North Carolina Capitol in 1948. *Author's collection.*

Andrew Jackson, Seventh President

The birthplace of Andrew Jackson is debatable. He was born someplace near Waxhaw in 1767. Whether it was in North Carolina or South Carolina is unknown, and both states claim him as one of their own. Jackson was captured during the American Revolution and then worked in a saddler's shop and taught school before studying law in Salisbury under Spruce Macay. While a young lawyer on the circuit, he often stayed at the Carson House (McDowell County). His first duel was fought with Waightstill Avery outside Jonesborough, now in Tennessee, in 1788. Jackson eventually settled in Tennessee, representing the state in the U.S. House and U.S. Senate. In 1814, he became a major general in the U.S. Army, successfully leading his troops against the British at the Battle of New Orleans in January 1815. In 1829, Jackson was elected president of the United States, serving until 1837.

Jackson's legacy as president is complicated. He was able to confront the nullification of South Carolina, keeping the Union together. Yet he also signed the Indian Removal Act, forcing the relocation of several Native American tribes, including the Cherokees, from the South. In 1832, he vetoed the corporate charter of the Second Bank of the United States, believing a national bank to be unconstitutional. Right before Jackson left office in March 1837, he recognized Texas's independence, setting up the state for annexation. Jackson returned to his home, the Hermitage, and passed away in 1845. There is a North Carolina Highway Historical Marker in Waxhaw commemorating his birth.

James K. Polk, Eleventh President

Often referred to as the first "dark horse" president, James K. Polk was born in Mecklenburg County in 1795. After graduating with honors from the University of North Carolina, he settled in Nashville, Tennessee, where he practiced law and became friends with Andrew Jackson. He served in the Tennessee House; the U.S. House, where he was Speaker from 1835 to 1839; and as governor of Tennessee. He was expecting a nomination as vice president in 1844, but when no consensus could be reached for the party's presidential pick, he was selected as the Democratic Party's presidential nominee.

Polk promised to serve only one term, a promise he kept. During his four years in office, Polk acquired vast territories along the Pacific coast and in the Southwest. Much of the property was purchased by the United States from Mexico after a highly unpopular war. The Department of the Interior, the U.S. Naval Academy and the Smithsonian Institution were all created during his time in office. While president, Polk visited Raleigh and Chapel Hill. After his one term ended in 1849, he returned to his home in Columbia, Tennessee, where he died on June 15, 1849. The James K. Polk Birthplace State Historic Site is located in Pineville. There are exhibits and displays concerning the life of Polk, with guided tours through reconstructed log buildings. A North Carolina Highway Historical Marker concerning Polk is located nearby.

Andrew Johnson, Seventeenth President

Born in Raleigh in 1808, Andrew Johnson was apprenticed to a tailor at the age of ten. At the age of fifteen, he ran away, heading first to Carthage and then to South Carolina. Johnson lived for a time in Knoxville, Tennessee, then Mooresville, Alabama, before settling in Greeneville, Tennessee, where he worked as a tailor. Johnson slowly rose through politics, serving as a town alderman, as mayor and in the Tennessee Statehouse, where he aligned with the Democrats. He served as a presidential elector in 1840 and then in the Tennessee Senate. In 1843, he was elected to the U.S. House, serving until 1853. That same year, he was elected governor of Tennessee, serving until 1857, when he was elected to the U.S. Senate.

Johnson was the only sitting southern senator who did not resign his seat when the Civil War came. Once Johnson's term ended in March 1862, President Abraham Lincoln appointed him military governor of Tennessee. In 1864, Lincoln went a step further, selecting the Democrat as his vice presidential running mate. The pair won by a landslide, and in March 1865, they were sworn into office. Six weeks later, Lincoln was assassinated in a Washington, D.C., theater, and Johnson was sworn in as the seventeenth president. With few Democrats in Congress, Johnson struggled with the Radical Republicans. While Johnson tried to adopt much of Lincoln's rather conciliatory plan for the restoration of the Union, the Republicans implemented much harsher terms. When Johnson attempted to dismiss Secretary of War Edwin Stanton, the House impeached Johnson. He was found not guilty by one vote in the Senate. Johnson failed to win the 1868 Democratic presidential nomination and returned to Tennessee. In 1875, he was elected for another term in the U.S. Senate but only served five months before he died.

In the Mordecai Historic Park in Raleigh is the Andrew Johnson Birthplace, a small structure that many believe to the birthplace of the president. It was moved to the park in 1975. There is a North Carolina Highway Historical Marker nearby.

VICE PRESIDENTS

William R. King is probably not a name that comes up very often. He served the shortest term of any vice president who did not become president of the United States. His term lasted just forty-five days. King was born in Sampson County in 1786. He graduated from the University of North Carolina in 1803 and then studied law under Judge William Duffy in Fayetteville. After one term in the General Assembly, and after serving as solicitor for Wilmington, King was elected to the U.S. House in 1811, serving three terms. He then served as the secretary for the U.S. minister to Russia in 1816–18. Upon his return, he headed west to Alabama. After building one of the largest plantations in the state, he was elected to the Alabama Statehouse, then the state senate, then the U.S. Senate; he served as minister to France and, finally, came back to the U.S. Senate. In 1851, the Democratic National Convention nominated Franklin Pierce for president and William King as vice president. They won the election. However, as King was ill with tuberculosis, he was not in the United States at the time. He had traveled to Cuba looking to regain his health. A special act of Congress allowed him to take his Oath of Office outside the United States, the only vice president to take the oath on foreign soil. King returned to the United States and made his way to Alabama, where he died on April 18, 1853, just forty-five days after becoming vice president. He is buried in Selma, Alabama. There is a North Carolina Highway Historical Marker at Monks Crossroads, Sampson County, that commemorates his life.

North Carolina native William R. King served less than two months as Franklin Pierce's vice president. *Library of Congress.*

FIRST LADY

Dolley Payne Madison, born in Guilford County, is North Carolina's only first lady. *Library of Congress.*

Dolley Payne Madison is North Carolina's only first lady. Her family had moved to the Quaker settlement of "New Garden," in Guilford County, when she was born on May 20, 1768. In 1769, the family returned to Virginia. She married John Todd in 1790 in Philadelphia. A yellow fever epidemic in 1793 killed her husband, son William and her in-laws. Dolley was possibly introduced to James Madison in May 1794 by Aaron Burr. Madison was a delegate at the nation's capital. They were married in September. Madison went on to serve as secretary of state for President Thomas Jefferson, and at times, Dolley served as hostess at the White House at ceremonial functions. Madison was elected president following Jefferson's two terms. During the War of 1812, Dolley saved a painting of Washington as the British arrived to burn the White House. Following Madison's tenure as president, the family retired to Montpelier. After the death of her husband, she returned to Washington, living there until her death in 1849. Dolley and the president are both buried at Montpelier. There is a North Carolina Highway Historical Marker in Greensboro commemorating her birth.

ALSO-RANS

Nathaniel Macon (1757–1837) represented North Carolina in both houses of Congress and served as Speaker of the House from 1801 to 1807. Macon opposed the ratification of the U.S. Constitution. In 1824, he received several electoral votes for vice president. There is a North Carolina Highway Historical Marker in Warren County commemorating his life.

Hugh Lawson White (1773–1840) was born in Iredell County but moved with his family to Tennessee. He served in the Tennessee Statehouse, in the state senate and as a judge. In 1825, he was appointed a U.S. senator. White broke with Andrew Jackson and the Democrats and became a Whig in 1836.

The Whig Party ran four candidates in the 1836 presidential election, and White came in third.

William Smith's (circa 1762–1840) birthplace is unclear, as it was either in North Carolina or South Carolina. A school friend of Andrew Jackson's, Smith served in the South Carolina Senate and as a judge prior to being appointed to the U.S. Senate in 1816. In 1828, seven electors from Georgia chose him for vice president over John C. Calhoun. In 1836, he came within one vote of being vice president. Smith later moved to Alabama, serving in the statehouse for a number of years. In 1837, Andrew Jackson nominated Smith as a Supreme Court justice. Smith was confirmed by the Senate but declined the appointment.

William A. Graham (1804–1875) was born in Lincoln County and graduated from the University of North Carolina. Graham practiced law in Hillsborough and was a member of the Whig Party. He served in the statehouse, in the U.S. Senate and as governor of North Carolina from 1845 to 1849. He then served as secretary of the navy under President Millard Fillmore. In 1852, the Whig Party nominated Winfield Scott and Graham as its presidential and vice presidential candidates, but they lost the campaign. After returning to North Carolina, Graham served in the state senate. Some suggested that Graham run for president in the Constitutional Union Party in 1860 and for governor in 1862. Graham declined. Graham was a Unionist member of the Secession Convention in 1861 and a representative at the Hampton Roads Conference in February 1865. It was Graham and former governor David L. Swain who surrendered Raleigh to William T. Sherman in April 1865. Graham was again elected to the U.S. Senate but was denied his seat by the Radicals. He was a driving force in North Carolina politics but did not hold office again until he was elected a delegate to the Constitutional Convention of 1875. He died before it assembled, however. There are North Carolina Highway Historical Markers in Lincoln County near his birthplace and in Hillsborough near his home. The gardens of the Graham home, Montrose, in Hillsborough are occasionally open for tours.

Joseph Lane (1801–1881) was born in Buncombe County. He was a descendant of Joel Lane, who sold the one thousand acres on which the capital of Raleigh was created. Three years later, the family moved to Kentucky. Lane moved to Indiana, where he became a prominent tradesman. He served several terms in the Indiana legislature and commanded a brigade during the Mexican-American War. After the war, President James K. Polk appointed Lane governor of the Territory of Oregon. He went on to serve several terms in the U.S. House and then the

Nathaniel Macon (*left*), William A. Graham and Joseph Lane all had aspirations for higher office. *State Archives of North Carolina* and *Library of Congress.*

U.S. Senate. In 1860, Lane became the vice presidential nominee beside then vice president John C. Breckinridge. The Breckinridge-Lane ticket came in second behind the Abraham Lincoln–Hannibal Hamlin ticket. Lane retired to Oregon following the election. There is a North Carolina Highway Historical Marker located in Asheville.

John Edwards (1953–present) was born in South Carolina and graduated from North Carolina State University and the University of North Carolina School of Law. He practiced law in Tennessee and North Carolina. Edwards was elected to the U.S. Senate in 1998, serving one term. In 2004, he became the Democratic vice presidential running mate of John Kerry. The pair lost to Republicans George W. Bush and Dick Cheney.

Further Reading:

Walter Borneman, *Polk: The Man Who Transformed the Presidency and America* (2009)

William Dodd, *Life of Nathaniel Macon* (2017)

John Meacham, *American Lion: Andrew Jackson in the White House* (2009)

Hans Trefousse, *Andrew Johnson: A Biography* (1997)

FIRST IN FREEDOM

THE AMERICAN REVOLUTION

The 1770s and 1780s were pivotal times in history. Tensions over taxes, lack of representation in Parliament and hostility between British soldiers and colonists led to war. In 1776, the state of North Carolina was formed and, with twelve other former colonies, created the United States of America. North Carolina played a pivotal role in the war that followed, as Great Britain tried to keep the colonies as a part of the British empire.

COASTAL

Moores Creek National Battlefield, Pender County

Now considered a minor battle of the American Revolution, the February 27, 1776 battle at Moore's (or Moores) Creek was an important battle early in the war. Royal Governor Josiah Martin was attempting to keep North Carolina loyal to the British. He had requested regular British soldiers to come and support local Loyalist forces. On their way to meet the British forces, 1,600 Loyalists attacked 1,100 Patriots at Moore's Creek Bridge. The Patriot forces were led by Richard Caswell, one of the first members of the Continental Congress and soon-to-be first governor of the state of North Carolina. The Patriot victory ended British authority in the colony, inspiring North Carolina to become the first colony to declare independence from Britain. The first battlefield property was preserved by the state in

Dedicated in 1907, the Moores Creek Women's Monument honors the women of the lower Cape Fear River area during the American Revolution. *Author's collection.*

1897. Later, the Moores Creek National Battlefield Park was authorized by Congress in 1944, and the enlarged property was transferred to the National Park Service. Within the park is a visitors' center and museum, and there are walking trails and markers located throughout the park. Visitors can hike part of the 1776 road that Patriot and Loyalist forces used. There are several North Carolina Highway Historical Markers in the area tied to the battle. These include "Moore's Camp," near Fayetteville; "Tory Rendezvous," northwest of Carthage; and "Moore's Creek Bridge," northeast of Currie.

Edenton Tea Party, Chowan County

One of Great Britain's attempts to generate income to pay for the French and Indian War was a tax on tea. This upset many colonists, who complained that since they were not represented in Parliament, they could not be taxed by those in London, only by their own general assemblies. In protest, Patriots dumped tea into Boston Harbor on December 16, 1773. Word of their

The British press ridiculed the ladies of Edenton after the women pledged to buy no British-made goods. *State Archives of North Carolina.*

actions spread across the colonies, and Patriots up and down the coast also dumped tea as a sign of protest. In North Carolina, fifty-one ladies met in Edenton on October 25, 1774. Led by Penelope Baker, they drafted a series of resolutions in which they stated they were boycotting not just British tea but textiles as well. The British press ridiculed the ladies in a cartoon that appeared in January 1775. There is a North Carolina Highway Historical Marker concerning the Edenton Tea Party in Edenton, along with one near the home of Baker. There is a plaque commemorating the event in the rotunda at the North Carolina Capitol in Raleigh, and the Edenton Tea Pot Memorial is located on the grounds of the Chowan County Courthouse.

Resolved…

In the eighteenth century, public gatherings in which a committee wrote a series of resolutions voicing approval or dissatisfaction over certain events were common occurrences. One of the most intriguing might have taken place on May 20, 1775. A group of citizens meeting in Charlotte, upon hearing of the Battles of Lexington and Concord, drew up a resolution declaring themselves "a free and independent people." This represents the first time any place in the colonies made such a bold more. However, no original copy of the Mecklenburg Declaration exists today, and many doubt that the document ever existed. Regardless, the date is important and has been for decades. May 20, 1775, appears on the state flag and the standard state license plate. Another document that can be proven did originate in Charlotte. On May 31, 1775, the Mecklenburg County Committee of Safety passed the Mecklenburg Resolves, declaring that the British laws were null and void in North Carolina. North Carolina was the first colony to take such a step. Captain Jack James is reported to have delivered the Mecklenburg Resolves to the Continental Congress. There is a monument to Captain Jack in Charlotte. Almost a year later, in Halifax, while the Fourth Provincial Congress was meeting, the delegates authorized the representatives meeting in Philadelphia at the Continental Congress to vote for independence. The date was April 12, 1776, and the document is known as the Halifax Resolves. There is a plaque in the North Carolina Capitol commemorating the Halifax Resolves. Also, there is a North Carolina Highway Historical Marker in Halifax as well as a monument.

First Provincial Congress, Craven County

There were five provincial congresses that gathered in North Carolina. The first met in New Bern in 1774. John Harvey (1724–1775) served as the first president. Harvey is often described as one of the most dynamic leaders and an outspoken opponent to British policies in North Carolina. There is a North Carolina Highway Historical Marker to Harvey in Herford. The First Provincial Congress was formed after the Boston Tea Party and had seventy-one delegates. There is a North Carolina Highway Historical Marker commemorating that First Provincial Congress in New Bern. The Second Provincial Congress was also held in New Bern. The Third, Fourth and Fifth Provincial Congresses were held in Hillsborough. The Fourth Provincial Congress approved the Halifax Resolves. The Fifth Provincial Congress approved the constitution for the new state of North Carolina and elected Richard Caswell as the state's first governor.

Battle of Elizabethtown, Bladen County

When the British captured Wilmington in January 1781, Tory forces became emboldened throughout the eastern counties. Tories raided farms, and Patriot forces found refuge in local woods and swamps. Elizabethtown seemed to be the center of Tory activity. Some four hundred Tory soldiers were stationed there. In August 1781, outnumbered Patriot forces crossed the Cape Fear River and attacked the Tory camp. Using cunning deception, after an initial volley, the Patriots called for the advance of phantom companies. Many of the Tories fled into a deep ravine, henceforth known as "Tory Hole." The Patriots' attack and ruse were successful. There is a monument on the grounds of the Bladen County Courthouse and a North Carolina Highway Historical Marker nearby.

Fort Johnston, Brunswick County

When Royal Governor Josiah Martin chose to flee the Governor's Mansion in New Bern, he went to Fort Johnston in Southport (then Smithville). Fort Johnston was built in 1744 on the western bank of the Cape Fear River. In July 1775, Patriot forces captured the fort, destroying it, while Governor Martin fled to a British sloop of war at anchor in the river. Patriot forces attempted to rebuild the fort in 1778. The British probably destroyed what had been built when they captured the area in 1781. The fort was later rebuilt during the Civil War and used by Confederate forces who renamed it Fort Branch and then Fort Pender. The area was occupied off and on until 2004. Today, Fort Johnson is composed of just one remaining building, which houses the Southport Museum and Visitor Center. There is a North Carolina Highway Historical Marker at the site.

Stamp Act, Brunswick County

When the Stamp Act passed the British Parliament in 1765, there were protests all across the colonies. According to the law, just about all paper products in the colonies—including cards, legal and business documents, licenses and materials published within the colonies—had to have stamps affixed to them. Colonists believed that only their state general assemblies had the right to tax them. In North Carolina, there were protests in New Bern, Cross Creek (Fayetteville), Edenton and Wilmington. In Wilmington, the Earl of Bute was burned in effigy. At one point, Governor William Tryon closed the port at Wilmington, insisting the act be enforced. Three ships sailing into the port of Wilmington were seized by the British in early 1766. Angry citizens seized the customshouse in Brunswick town and Fort Johnston. In February, two of the ships were allowed to proceed to their destinations. In March 1766, the British Parliament repealed the Stamp Act. There are several North Carolina Highway Historical Markers in the eastern portion of North Carolina that commemorate subjects related to the event. These include the Stamp Act marker in Belville; Russellborough, at the Brunswick Town State Historic Site in Brunswick County, home of Governor Tryon; stampmaster William Houston, northeast of Kenansville, Duplin County; Old Courthouse in Wilmington; and General John Ashe, north of Rocky Point, Pender County.

Brunswick Town, Brunswick County

The town of Brunswick was a major port on the Cape Fear River prior to the American Revolution. The town was founded in 1726 and named for the Duke of Brunswick, King George I. Tar, pitch, turpentine and other naval stores were all shipped from the port. It was also the home to two

St. Phillip's Episcopal Church in Brunswick, constructed in 1768, was burned by the British in 1776. *State Archives of North Carolina.*

royal governors, Arthur Dobbs and William Tryon. The house where they lived was named Russellborough. The home and much of the town were razed by the British in 1776. Confederate forces built Fort Anderson at the site during the 1860s. Archaeological excavation began at the site in the late 1950s. Brunswick Town/Fort Anderson State Historic Site displays locally recovered cannons and artifacts in the visitors' center/museum. There are North Carolina Highway Historical Markers for Brunswick, Russellborough and St. Phillip's Church nearby.

PIEDMONT

Guilford Court House National Military Park, Guilford County

Following the Battle of Kings Mountain, the British forces retreated from Charlotte and moved back into South Carolina for several months. Following the defeat of Colonel Banastre Tarleton at Cowpens, South Carolina, Cornwallis gave chase to the victorious Patriot forces, moving into North Carolina in January 1781. Patriot forces were under the command of General Nathanael Greene, who conducted a tactical retreat across the

The most impressive monument on the Guilford Court House Battlefield is to Nathanael Greene, commander of the Patriot forces. *Author's collection.*

state, drawing the British from their base of supplies into an area with sparse supplies. The reinforced Patriot army met the British in battle at Guilford Court House. While the British were victorious, the campaign seriously weakened their army. Cornwallis moved to Wilmington, and then, in April 1781, moved to Yorktown, Virginia, where on October 19, surrounded by American and French forces, he surrendered. Work on preserving the battleground began in 1887, when the Guilford Battleground Company was formed. By 1917, the organization was able to turn over 125 acres to the new Guilford Court House National Military Park. The park contains a visitors' center with a museum, numerous monuments and walking trails. There is also a North Carolina Highway Historical Marker located nearby.

Signers' Monument, Guilford County

North Carolina sent seventeen delegates to represent the state in the Continental Congress between 1774 and 1789. Three of those—Edenton's Joseph Hewes, Granville County's John Penn and New Hanover County's William Hooper—signed the Declaration of Independence in 1776. All three are honored with a plaque inside the North Carolina Capitol in Raleigh. On the Guilford Court House Battlefield in Greensboro is a monument to two of those signers. Often called the Signers' Monument, the statue pays homage to Hooper and Penn and was erected in 1897. The Joseph Hewes Memorial is located on the grounds of the Chowan County Courthouse in Edenton. It was dedicated in 1932. There is also a North Carolina Highway Historical Marker in Edenton to Hewes, one in Wilmington near the home of Hooper and one in Granville three miles from the home of Penn. The marker to Penn is the very first highway marker erected by the state. John Penn (1740–1788) and William Hooper (1742–1790) are now interred on the grounds of Guilford Court House Battlefield. Joseph Hewes is buried in Philadelphia.

MOUNTAINS

Overmountain Victory National Historic Trail

Both Thomas Jefferson and Theodore Roosevelt considered the Battle of Kings Mountain the turning point of the American Revolution. By 1780, British forces had captured much of South Carolina, and they were poised to sweep through North Carolina, rallying Loyalists to the king's standard. British commander Lord Cornwallis entered Charlotte on September 26. To protect his western flank, Cornwallis dispatched Colonel Patrick Ferguson to suppress dissidents in the foothill regions. Ferguson sent a message to the leaders of the settlements on the other side of the Blue Ridge Mountains, demanding the leaders surrender or Ferguson would march into the area and destroy their farms and communities. The militias from the area responded, meeting Ferguson and his Loyalist forces at Kings Mountain on the North Carolina/South Carolina border and utterly defeating them. Ferguson was killed in the ensuing battle. While there were militia companies from Virginia and South Carolina, the bulk came from Surry and Wilkes Counties and from Washington and Sullivan Counties, then in North Carolina but now in Tennessee. There are many sites and markers to commemorate this important event. The 330-mile Overmountain Victory Trail is a commemorative motor trail that covers four different states. It traces the route of the Overmountain Men on their way to Kings Mountain. There are North Carolina Highway Historical Markers at the Surry Muster Field in Elkin, Quaker Meadows in Morganton and Gilbert Town near Rutherfordton. Patrick Ferguson has

Located at the Museum of North Carolina Minerals, Spruce Pine, this marker denotes the site of Gillespie Gap, a camping site for the Overmountain Men. *Author's collection.*

a marker in Grover, and one for the Battle of Kings Mountain is in Kings Mountain. The Kings Mountain Historical Museum has exhibits on the area and the battle. Just a few miles south of the North Carolina state line is the Kings Mountain National Military Park.

Further Reading:

Daniel W. Barefoot, *Touring North Carolina's Revolutionary War Sites* (1998)

Jeff Broadwater and Troy L. Kickler, eds., *North Carolina's Revolutionary Founders* (2019)

Hugh F. Rankin, *North Carolina in the American Revolution* (1965, 2016)

FIRST, FARTHEST AND LAST

THE CIVIL WAR

At first, North Carolina resisted the call to war in 1861. Many of the citizens were content to remain in the Union. Yet with the firing on Fort Sumter in neighboring South Carolina and President Abraham Lincoln's call for 75,000 troops to put down the rebellion, North Carolina joined with the other Southern states in a new nation, the Confederate States of America. Men and companies from across the state poured into training camps in Raleigh, Asheville, High Point and Wilmington. By June 1861, Tar Heel soldiers were in neighboring Virginia, fighting the first land battle of the war at Big Bethel. Eventually, 125,000 men from North Carolina joined Confederate ranks, taking part in all the major battles east of the Mississippi River. Traditionally, 40,000 North Carolinians are believed to have lost their lives during the war. The phrase "First, Farthest and Last" has often been used to describe North Carolina's pivotal role in the war: first at the Battle of Big Bethel, farthest at Gettysburg and Chickamauga and last at Appomattox.

North Carolina was not a homogenous entity during the war. There were thousands who still favored the Union and thousands more who aligned with neither side. The war was more than just men marching away to fight and die on distant fields in Virginia, Georgia and Tennessee. It affected every family and every corner of the state. The North Carolina Museum of History in Raleigh has an extensive collection of artifacts that belonged to the soldiers from the state and is a great place to begin exploring.

On April 27, 1861, Lincoln ordered a blockade of Southern ports, including those in North Carolina, although the state did not vote to leave the Union until May 20, 1861. While there were many port towns along North Carolina's coast, few of them boasted harbors deep enough for large ships. The Cape Fear River and the town of Wilmington provided the primary port for both shipping out commodities like cotton and receiving munitions of war such as rifles, cannons, powder, medicines and foodstuffs. To protect the Cape Fear River, Confederate forces constructed Fort Fisher and Fort Anderson and strengthened existing forts such as Fort Caswell on Oak Island. Fort Caswell is privately owned today, but the other two are state historic sites open to the public: Fort Fisher State Historic Site and Brunswick Town/Fort Anderson. The Cape Fear Museum in Wilmington has several exhibits telling the story of the area. Eventually, Fort Fisher was bombarded and captured in January 1865, closing the last major port city in the East.

Following secession, state forces seized Federal installations, such as lighthouses, along with Fort Macon near Beaufort, the arsenal in Fayetteville and the U.S. Mint in Charlotte. The lights from the lighthouses were removed, the arsenal began manufacturing rifles for the Confederate government and the mint building largely sat empty. Only two of the original lighthouses still stand: Ocracoke Light Station on Ocracoke Island and Old Baldy on Bald Head Island. The arsenal was destroyed by Federal forces in March 1865. Remains of the arsenal can be found at the North Carolina Civil War & Reconstruction History Center in Fayetteville. The U.S. Mint building in Charlotte was used to house the Confederate treasury in the last days of the war but was never utilized to mint coins after the conflict. Today, the Mint Museum Randolph houses an art museum.

Federal forces were quick to capture the Outer Banks. A fort on Hatteras Island was captured in August, and Fort Ocracoke was abandoned in September. In February 1862, Federal forces fought and captured Roanoke Island and, in March, took New Bern, giving them control of the Pamlico Sound for the rest of the war. There are historical markers on Roanoke Island, and a portion of the battlefield has been preserved at the New Bern Civil War Battlefield Park. Following New Bern, Federals laid siege to Fort Macon, which capitulated on April 26, 1862. The brick-masonry fort, one of two in North Carolina, is preserved and can be visited at Fort Macon State Park.

With such a foothold in Eastern North Carolina, Federal forces could make drives farther into the interior of the state. Cutting the Wilmington and Weldon Railroad was vital. In December 1862, Federals launched a raid

In March 1862, the fall of New Bern opened much of Eastern North Carolina to Federal attacks. *State Archives of North Carolina.*

toward Goldsboro in an effort to cut the railroad. This resulted in battles at Kinston and Seven Springs. Another raid took place in July 1863, with Federal forces hitting Greenville, Tarboro and Rocky Mount.

In January 1864, Confederate forces attempted to wrest control of Eastern North Carolina from the Federals. An attempt to capture New Bern was met with defeat. However, Confederate forces attacked by both land and water, capturing Plymouth in April, which in turn forced the evacuation of Washington. A second attempt in early May 1864 to capture New Bern was also unsuccessful when the attacking Confederate forces were ordered to return to Virginia.

One of the Confederate vessels participating in the attacks at Plymouth and New Bern was the CSS *Albemarle*, known as the "Cornfield Ironclad" due to its construction in a cornfield on the Roanoke River. On the night of October 27, 1864, a small group of Federal sailors worked their way up to the *Albemarle* and, under the cover of darkness, drove a torpedo into the side of the ship. The resulting explosion sent the ship to the bottom of the river. After the war, the *Albemarle* was raised, towed to Virginia, condemned as a prize and then sold for scrap. One of the cannons from the *Albemarle* is in Norfolk, while the ship's bell is displayed at the Museum of the Albemarle in Elizabeth City, and the smokestack is at the Port O' Plymouth Museum in Plymouth.

Fort Macon was captured by the Confederates at the beginning of the war and then recaptured by the Federals in 1862. *State Archives of North Carolina.*

At the end of December, Federal naval and land forces attempted to capture Fort Fisher. On Christmas Eve, naval forces bombarded the fort, while the next day, infantry prepared to storm the fortifications. However, the attacking column, already on the beach, was called back to the ships and steamed north. The first attack ended in failure. A new commander was appointed, and a second attack commenced on January 13, 1865. This time, the fort was captured, and the last major port open in the East was closed. The closed port prevented supplies from flowing as before and crippled the Confederate army in Virginia. Fort Caswell was abandoned, and Fort Anderson was captured after a brief battle. Wilmington was captured on February 22.

Federal forces advancing west out of New Bern ran into Confederate soldiers near Kinston on March 8. In a battle that lasted a few days, Confederate forces were able to capture part of the Federal lines and about one thousand men, but the arrival of reinforcements forced the Confederates to abandon their position. Scuttled as they retreated was the

CSS *Neuse*, an ironclad being built in the area. In 1963, the CSS *Neuse* was raised and the hull put on display. Visitors can see the hull and learn more about the war in the area by visiting the CSS *Neuse* Civil War Interpretive Center in Kinston.

In December 1864, Federal soldiers under General William T. Sherman completed their March to the Sea when they reached Savannah. The Federals then turned north, beginning a march through the Carolinas. By March 8, Federal forces under Sherman were crossing the Pee Dee River into North Carolina. Cavalry commands visited and plundered towns like Wadesboro and Lumberton. On March 10, cavalry elements from both commands clashed at Monroe's Crossroads in Cumberland County. The following day, Federal forces entered Fayetteville. While in the town, they burned several important textile mills, the newspaper office and, eventually, the arsenal itself, although the Confederates had already transported much of the machinery to the Egypt Coal Mine in Lee County.

Confederate forces continued to fight delaying actions such as the one at Averasboro on March 15–16, slowing portions of the Federal army's advance. A portion of the field is preserved, and more information can be found at the Averasboro Battlefield Museum near Dunn. The main Confederate army in

The capture of Fort Fisher in January 1865 closed the last major port open to the Confederacy. *Library of Congress.*

the state, remnants of the Army of Tennessee and some Confederates from Wilmington and other garrisons, clashed with the Federals at Bentonville March 19–21, 1865. Initially, the Confederates were successful in pushing back the Federals. But with reinforcement, the Federals were able to stabilize their lines, and the Confederates fell back toward Raleigh. Bentonville is the state's largest Civil War battlefield and its best preserved. The Bentonville Battlefield State Historic Site is located in Johnston County.

While the western part of the state had been engaged in an internecine civil war for much of 1863 and 1864, pitting neighbors against one another and, at times, against pro-Confederate, pro-Union and dissident factions, Federal soldiers finally made more serious military attempts in 1865. In February 1865, a Federal force attempted to attack Asheville but was beaten, retreating to Tennessee. Informational plaques regarding the failed Federal efforts can be found at the University of North Carolina–Asheville's Botanical Gardens.

In early spring 1865, a Federal cavalry force under Major General George Stoneman launched a raid through the northwestern part of the state. On March 28, the troopers skirmished in Boone with the home guard and then proceeded east through portions of Caldwell and Wilkes Counties. They turned in the direction of Virginia for several days before crossing back into North Carolina on April 9. The main force moved through Winston and Salem, while detachments spread out toward Greensboro. At Salisbury on April 12, the Federals ran into Confederates manning breastworks. They eventually flanked the Confederates out of their entrenchments and won the day. An attempt to burn the high bridge over the Yadkin River on the Rowan-Davie County border did not go as well, and Stoneman, after burning supplies and the old Salisbury Prison, moved toward the west. On April 13, they passed through Statesville, wrecking the newspaper office and burning the depot and nearby supplies. Stoneman and an estimated one thousand prisoners passed through Lenoir and back into Boone, while the remainder of the column moved farther west toward Morganton and Asheville. The Federals passed through Asheville peacefully, but upon hearing of Lincoln's assassination, they turned back and sacked the town. Information on Stoneman's Raid can be found in numerous local history museums, such as the Wilkes Heritage Museum in Wilkesboro, the Rowan Museum in Salisbury, the Caldwell Historical Museum in Lenoir and the Museum of Burke County History in Morganton. There are also numerous North Carolina Highway Historical Markers and Civil War Trail Markers found tracing the route in several counties.

The largest surrender of Confederate soldiers during the war took place at the Bennett Farm, just outside Durham. *Author's collection.*

In the eastern part of the state, the Federals followed the Confederates through Raleigh. Many of the Confederate troops camped in Greensboro and High Point. The two army commanders met at the Bennett Farm near Durham for several days in late April 1865. They eventually worked out the details that led to the largest surrender of Confederate forces during the war. Almost ninety thousand Confederate soldiers were paroled and sent toward their homes across the South. The event is remembered at the Bennett Place State Historic Site in Durham.

For a brief time, while the commanders were working out the surrender details, North Carolina served as the capital of the Confederacy. Confederate president Jefferson Davis and his cabinet arrived in Greensboro on April 11. After remaining for a few days, his party moved south, passing through Lexington, Salisbury and Concord. They arrived in Charlotte on April 19 and set up offices in the newspaper building. When the terms between the armies were settled, making no mention of the disposition of civil officials, Davis held one final meeting of the Confederate cabinet at the Phifer home and then left. With a cavalry escort and a few of the cabinet members, Jefferson departed Charlotte on April 26, crossing over the Catawba River and into South Carolina. The whole cabinet would never meet again, and

Wartime governor Zebulon Baird Vance was born on these grounds in a similar modest log cabin. *Author's collection.*

Davis was captured in Georgia on May 10. There are North Carolina Highway Historical Markers denoting the route in Greensboro, near Lexington, Concord and Charlotte.

North Carolina's role in the Civil War is vast and complex, and there are, of course, many other sites that commemorate the period. There are almost two hundred Civil War Trail Markers in North Carolina, from Robbinsville to Knott's Island, that give visitors details about this fascinating piece of North Carolina's history. Worthy of a visit is the Vance Birthplace State Historic Site near Weaverville, the childhood home of wartime governor Zebulon Baird Vance, and *Boundless*, the memorial to United States Colored Troops, on the grounds of the Cameron Art Museum in Wilmington.

Further Reading:

John G. Barrett, *The Civil War in North Carolina* (1963)
Michael C. Hardy, *North Carolina in the Civil War* (2011)
Clint Johnson, *Touring the Carolina's Civil War Sites* (1996)

"OVER THERE!"

WORLD WAR I

It was called the Great War—the War to End All Wars. While it was great in scale, World War I was, unfortunately, not the war to end all wars. It would only precipitate future conflicts. President Woodrow Wilson tried to keep the United States out of the European war. But with attempted German intervention in Mexico and the Caribbean, coupled with the sinking of U.S. merchant vessels by German submarines, the United States was finally forced to declare war on the Central Powers in April 1917. North Carolina played a vital role in that conflict, both at home and with troops sent overseas. North Carolina sent 86,457 men and women to fight, build bridges and roads, haul supplies and minister to the wounded and sick. In just five months, 624 North Carolinians were killed, 3,655 were wounded (of which 204 later died) and 1,542 died of disease.

MEDAL OF HONOR WINNERS

Three native-born North Carolinians earned the Medal of Honor for exemplary service during World War I. They are Robert L. Blackwell (Person County), Samuel I. Parker (Union County) and Henry Johnson (Forsyth County). Johnson moved to New York prior to the war and served with the legendary Harlem Hellfighters. He passed away in 1929 and is buried at Arlington National Cemetery. Samuel I. Parker is considered the most highly decorated U.S. Army soldier of World War I. A second lieutenant, Parker earned not only the Medal of Honor but also the Distinguished Service Cross, two Silver Stars, two Purple Hearts and other awards. Following World War I, he worked in the textile industry and trained soldiers at Fort Benning, Georgia, during World War II. He is buried at Oakwood Cemetery, Concord. There is a North Carolina Highway Historical Marker for Parker in Monroe. Robert L. Blackwell served with the 119th Infantry, 30th Division. He was killed on October 11, 1918, while trying to relay a message after his platoon was pinned down by enemy troops. Blackwell is buried at the Somme American Cemetery in France and is honored with a North Carolina Highway Historical Marker southwest of Roxboro and a monument on the grounds of the Person County Courthouse, Roxboro.

IMPORTANT CONTRIBUTORS

Several North Carolina natives made important contributions to the war by serving in high-level positions. These men have North Carolina Highway Historical Markers to tell their stories. U.S. Senator Furnifold M. Simmons, chair of the Senate Committee on Finance, has two markers: one near Pollocksville (Jones County) that notes the place of his birth and another in New Bern that commemorates the site of his home. Walter H. Pines was a newspaper editor and partner at Doubleday, Page and Company prior to being appointed ambassador to the United Kingdom by President Woodrow Wilson. There is not only a memorial plaque to him in Westminster Abbey in London but also markers denoting his place of birth in Cary and his grave site in Aberdeen. Samson L. Faison achieved the rank of brigadier general during World War I and played a significant role in breaking the Hindenburg Line in Germany. There is a marker denoting his birthplace in Faison.

COASTAL

Camp Glenn, Carteret County

The origins of Camp Glenn date back to 1906, when the General Assembly established a training camp for National Guard soldiers headed to the

U.S.-Mexican border. The camp was named for former governor Robert B. Glenn. In 1918, the camp was acquired by the U.S. Navy and became an air station. There is a North Carolina Highway Historical Marker in Morehead City.

PIEDMONT

Camp Polk, Wake County

In September 1918, as part of the nationwide mobilization effort, the federal government established Camp Polk in Raleigh. The camp was named in honor of Colonel William Polk, an officer during the American Revolution. The temporary camp became a training school for newly introduced tanks. When the armistice came on November 11, 1918, the camp was closed. Soldiers were housed in tents, and few of the planned buildings were completed. Later, the Camp Polk Prison Farm was located at this site.

Camp Polk, in Raleigh, was used as a World War I tank training camp. *State Archives of North Carolina.*

Camp Greene, Mecklenburg County

Once the United States entered World War I, camps were needed to train the hundreds of thousands of men mobilized to go and fight. One of the first camps established in North Carolina was Camp Greene in Charlotte. Named for Revolutionary War general Nathanael Greene, the camp encompassed 2,500 acres. There were thousands of buildings to house and care for the troops, plus a trench line to replicate the trenches in France. More than 40,000 troops were trained at Camp Greene, including 14,000 African Americans. Nothing of the camp remains today. There is a North Carolina Highway Historical Marker in Charlotte, along with a monument to the camp at the intersection of Wilkinson and Monument Streets.

Camp Bragg, Cumberland County

Camp Bragg was one of three U.S. Army camps established in North Carolina during World War I. It was named after Confederate general and North Carolina native Braxton Bragg. The base became the primary training location for artillery. Later, infantry arrived to train at the facility as well. The base nearly closed after the war, but by World War II, it had become the largest base in the United States. There is a North Carolina Highway Historical Marker on the base. Several museums in Fayetteville have information on the post and its role in history.

MOUNTAINS

German Internee Camp, Madison County

The start of World War I in July 1914 found thousands of German citizens living in the United States and under suspicion. Allowing German ships in U.S. ports to sail could cost many lives, so the United States detained these Germans. One thousand of them were placed in a camp in Madison County at the Hot Springs Hotel. The internees built additional structures, including a chapel, shops and even a carousel. The internees were eventually transferred to Georgia. Nothing remains today, but there is a North Carolina Highway Historical Marker in Hot Springs.

Right: The Camp Greene monument was dedicated in November 1926, marking the site of the camp that trained more than forty thousand men during World War I. *Brian Duckworth.*

Below: Camp Bragg was one of the primary artillery training camps during World War I. *State Archives of North Carolina.*

One thousand German detainees were held in a camp in Madison County. Nothing remains of the village they constructed. *State Archives of North Carolina.*

Kiffin Y. Rockwell, Buncombe County

The La Fayette Escadrille was a French air force unit composed mostly of American volunteer pilots. It was named in honor of the Marquis de Lafayette, French hero of the American Revolution. There were four North Carolinians in the group. Kiffin Y. Rockwell was one of those pilots. In May 1916, he became the first American to shoot down a German plane. Rockwell was killed in a dogfight on September 23, 1916, the second American to die in aerial combat. He is buried in France. There is a North Carolina Highway Trail Marker in Asheville near his boyhood home.

Further Reading:

Jessica A. Bandel, *North Carolina and the Great War, 1914–1918* (2017)

R. Jackson Marshall, *Memories of World War I: North Carolina Doughboys on the Western Front* (1998)

Shepherd W. McKinley and Steve Sabol, eds., *North Carolina's Experience During World War I* (2018)

NORTH CAROLINA'S "GREATEST GENERATION"

WORLD WAR II

World War II had a profound impact on the state of North Carolina. Most of the state's residents were rural, poor and still in the throes of the Great Depression. The war brought industry, new people and an economic stimulus to the state. Following the war, the GI Bill helped many veterans attend college, and a budget surplus allowed the state to continue to transform into a more urbanized society. There were numerous camps and posts constructed or enlarged across the state. By the end of the war, Fort Bragg had become the largest military post in the United States. More than 370,000 North Carolinians joined the military, including more than 7,000 women. Over 7,000 Tar Heels lost their lives in the conflict. At times, the war was right on the doorstep of the state, being waged in "Torpedo Alley" off the Outer Banks. Thousands of Italian and German prisoners were housed in North Carolina. Many wartime essentials, such as mica, were mined by the state. Tens of thousands worked in the war industry, while thousands of others volunteered with civil defense or the aircraft warning service, or contributed by donating to scrap drives, growing Victory Gardens or giving books to the Victory Book Campaign.

During World War II, patriotic scenes like this one at the Center Theater in Lenoir, Caldwell County, were found in every town across the state. *Caldwell Historical Museum.*

COASTAL

Greater Wilmington Area, New Hanover County

By 1943, Wilmington had grown from a prewar population of 33,400 to 120,000. The North Carolina Shipbuilding Company employed 21,000 people at its peak, producing 243 cargo and passenger ships during the war. Squadrons of P-39s, B-17s and B-24s were stationed at Bluethenthal Field (now Wilmington International Airport) and routinely made patrols up and down the coast, looking for German U-boats and surviving crew members of torpedoed ships. Pilots, mostly WASP (Women Airforce Service Pilots), frequently took off towing targets for anti-aircraft training at nearby Camp Davis. South of Wilmington is Fort Fisher. While better known for its role as a Confederate fortress, the area had a landing field and was used by anti-aircraft batteries as a training facility. Across the Cape Fear River, Fort

Caswell was used by the navy as a submarine tracking base, communications center and depot. At Kure Beach was the Ethyl Corporation. According to local tradition, the facility was supposedly attacked by a German submarine on June 25, 1943.

In 2020, Wilmington became the United States' first "World War II Heritage City." The highlight is the USS *North Carolina*, a 1941 battleship that saw action in the Pacific Theater of the war. Known as the "Showboat," the *North Carolina* was just one of forty-one naval vessels representing the state during the war. Decommissioned in June 1947, the ship was finally purchased by the state and, in April 1962, was opened as a war memorial. Tours and other experiences are provided at the USS *North Carolina*'s permanent berth in Wilmington.

There are numerous North Carolina Highway Historical Markers in the area, including one for the North Carolina Shipbuilding Company and one for the USS *North Carolina.* The Fort Fisher State Historic Site, Cape Fear Museum and the North Carolina Maritime Museum in Southport all have exhibits on the role of the area during World War II.

The SS *Zebulon Vance* was the first Liberty ship constructed in Wilmington during World War II. *State Archives of North Carolina.*

Holly Ridge, Pender County

Camp Davis was a Coast Artillery Camp established in 1941, training both White and Black artillery units and testing new anti-aircraft weapons. More than two thousand women were stationed at Camp Davis, including some of the WASP. The site is still an active military post, but there is a North Carolina Highway Historical Marker nearby. In 1946, the Topsail Firing Range, a part of Camp Davis, was acquired by the U.S. Navy, which used the area to test a top-secret ram-jet missile, known as "Operation Bumblebee." The Missiles and More Museum on Topsail Beach has exhibits and information on the program and on Camp Davis.

Morehead City/Beauford/Cape Lookout

During the war, Morehead City served as a base for Coast Guard and navy anti-submarine vessels, while the local hospital treated victims of U-boat attacks. Cape Lookout was considered a harbor for ships moving up the coast. The area was protected by an anti-submarine net and a mine field. Fort Macon was garrisoned by the 244th Coast Artillery. While the attacks by U-boats were out of range for those garrisoning Fort Macon, they could see the fires out to sea. Occasionally, portions of wrecked vessels were towed into Beaufort Inlet for salvage. There is a monument marking the site of the naval base at U.S. 70 and 35th Street in Morehead City. The North Carolina Maritime Museum in Beaufort also has exhibits on World War II in the area.

Elizabeth City, Pasquotank County

During the war, Elizabeth City had one of the largest Coast Guard air stations on the East Coast. Constructed nearby was the Weeksville Dirigible Hanger, an airship manufacturing, storage and test facility. Dirigibles were blimps used in anti-submarine patrols off the coast, from Delaware Bay to Charleston, South Carolina. Airships were ideal observation aircraft, given their ability to hover in one spot for extended lengths of time. One of the massive dirigible hangers still survives.

CAPE HATTERAS AREA

One of the largest mine fields laid by the U.S. Navy during World War II was located in the Cape Hatteras region. The military was trying to protect the merchant vessels plying the seas. The British Cemetery in Ocracoke contains the graves of four sailors who drowned when their vessel was torpedoed.

Jacksonville/New Bern

Camp Lejeune, established in 1941, trained tens of thousands of U.S. marines for a variety of roles during the war years. The camp had a separate facility for female marines and a facility to train "Devil Dogs," canines used to detect minefields or enemy troops. Montford Point, a separate camp to train African Americans (since the U.S. military was segregated at the time), opened in 1942. Nearby was the U.S. Marine Corps Air Station, Cherry Point. Considered one of the most expensive construction projects of World

African American engineers of the 51st Composite Battalion, U.S. Marine Corps, practice with .30-caliber machine guns on a range at Camp Lejeune. *Library of Congress.*

War II and one of the largest airfields in the world, Cherry Point provided advanced training to marine pilots. Both sites are still active military bases. President Roosevelt visited the post in 1944. There is a North Carolina Highway Historical Marker for Cherry Point in Havelock, one for Montfort Point in Jacksonville and one for Camp Lejeune in Jacksonville. There are several other memorials and monuments in the area, including the Montford Point Marine Memorial, the Beirut Memorial and the Vietnam Veterans Memorial, all located in the Lejeune Memorial Garden in Jacksonville.

PIEDMONT

Fayetteville, Cumberland County

Camp Bragg became Fort Bragg in 1921. The facility was home to the 9th Infantry Division and conducted all artillery training east of the Mississippi River. The first military parachute jumps were conducted here in 1923. In 1942, the post became home to the new airborne units and at its peak had 157,000 residents. The 4th Army Corps was trained here before its invasion of North Africa; the 82nd, 101st, 11th, 13th and 17th airborne divisions trained here or at nearby Camp Mackall; and the army's first all-Black parachute unit, the 555th Parachute Infantry Battalion, trained here as well. Fayetteville is home to several world-class museums, including the Airborne and Special Operations Museum, which features exhibits on the World War II airborne and later Special Forces units. The museum has an actual C-47 "Skytrain," a CG A4 glider and numerous displays of uniforms and weapons. The 82nd Airborne Division War Memorial Museum began in 1945 and traces the 82nd Division all the way back to World War I. There are numerous displays, including an airpark with a C-47, helicopters and a glider. There are also displays and exhibits that document the 82nd Airborne up to today. The North Carolina Veterans Park honors all North Carolina veterans. Artwork is made from recycled military ruins, the granite comes from Mount Airy, the plants are native varieties and there is soil from every North Carolina county. Also in Fayetteville is a North Carolina Highway Historical Marker to David M. Williams. "Carbine" Williams designed the floating chamber and the short-stroke piston used in the popular World War II–era M1 Carbine.

Raleigh/Durham

Ten miles northeast of Durham was Camp Butner. Established in 1942 as a training facility for the 35th and 78th Infantry, it also served as a hospital for wounded soldiers. At one time, the camp housed thirty-five thousand people, including five thousand German and Italian prisoners of war. The latter often worked for the military and local farmers. The Camp Butner Museum is located in the Soldiers Memorial Sports Arena in Butner, and a North Carolina Highway Historical Marker is nearby. The Raleigh-Durham International Airport was under construction in 1941 when it was taken over by the government and dubbed the Raleigh-Durham Army Air Base. The field was used for training. In Durham, on the campus of Duke University, is a monument to the members of the 65th General Hospital. These doctors and nurses pioneered revolutionary treatments for wounded soldiers.

Greensboro, Guilford County

The Greater Greensboro area was heavily involved in the war effort. Lindley Field was used as an aerial debarkation facility for troopers heading overseas and as a refueling stop for the air-ferry system. The airport was also used to train fighter and bomber pilots. The Army Air Force Basic Training Center No. 10 operated in Greensboro from March 1943 to May 1944. More than 87,500 men passed through the center, learning the basics of military life. Once that program closed, the base became an Overseas Replacement Depot for members of the U.S. Army Air Corps. Here airmen were processed, reassigned to new duties and often shipped overseas. A North Carolina Highway Historical Marker on Wendover Avenue marks the 652-acre site. Also in Greensboro is a North Carolina Highway Historical Marker for George Preddy, North Carolina's top fighter ace. He was credited with 26.83 kills before he himself was killed in a friendly-fire incident in December 1944. Preddy was born in Greensboro.

MOUNTAINS

Grove Park Inn, Buncombe County

The Greater Asheville area played an interesting role in the war effort. Many of the large hotels—including the Grove Park Inn, the George Vanderbilt,

Grove Park Inn, pictured here circa 1913, played a conspicuous role in World War II. *Library of Congress.*

the Asheville-Biltmore and the Battery Park—were used by the army as distribution centers, while the U.S. Army Air Corps used Lake Lure Inn and the Rocky Road Inn. Military personnel were given time to rest and relax, often with their families, before being reassigned. The Grove Park Inn also housed Axis diplomats from Italy, Hungry and Bulgaria while they awaited exchange for Allied diplomats. In the spring of 1944, the Inn served as the temporary headquarters of the exiled Philippine government. President Franklin D. Roosevelt and General Dwight D. Eisenhower visited as well. Also in the area was the Moore General Hospital, a 2,605-bed facility in Swannanoa, and the U.S. Naval Hospital, Kenilworth Park.

Further Reading:

Homer Hickam, *Torpedo Junction: U-Boat War off America's East Coast, 1942* (1989)

Julian M. Pleasants, *Home Front: North Carolina During World War II* (2017)

FROM ENSLAVEMENT TO THE STRUGGLE FOR EQUALITY

MILESTONES IN AFRICAN AMERICAN HISTORY

The struggle for civil rights in North Carolina is a lengthy, complicated and often painful history. There have been some remarkable people and events in North Carolina that represent important milestones in the journey of Black Americans to seek excellence and equality, despite often overwhelming opposition. A great place to begin exploring this subject is the International Civil Rights Center & Museum in Greensboro. The museum is housed in the Woolworth building that was the site of the pivotal Greensboro sits-ins in February 1960. After the closing of Woolworth, the building was slated for demolition. Local politicians stepped in and founded a nonprofit that purchased the property. The museum opened on February 1, 2010, the fiftieth anniversary of the sit-in. There are exhibits and artifacts from the events pertaining to the 1950s through the 1970s.

COASTAL

Washington Waterfront Underground Railroad Museum, Beaufort County

Housed in an old Seaboard Coast Line Railroad caboose in Washington, the Washington Underground Railroad Museum tells an important piece of North Carolina history: the plight of enslaved people attempting to escape to freedom through the eastern part of our state. The Great Dismal

Swamp was once home to the largest group of escaped slaves in the South. Many of these men and women utilized a route known as the Underground Railroad. It was a network of people, both White and Black, who offered aid and shelter to the enslaved attempting to get north, usually to Canada. The museum has numerous photographs and exhibits and is one of ten sites on the National Park Service's Network to Freedom Underground Railroad Locations in North Carolina.

James F. Shober, New Hanover County

Born enslaved in Salem, James F. Shober (1853–1889) was freed by the Thirteenth Amendment in December 1865. After graduating from Lincoln University and the Howard University School of Medicine, Shober settled in Wilmington and began to practice medicine. Shober was the first African American physician in North Carolina with a medical degree. There is a North Carolina Highway Historical Marker in Wilmington not far from his home and office.

Alex Manley, Wilmington Race Riot, New Hanover County

Tensions regarding race relationships in North Carolina, as in most states, were high in the years following the Civil War. For example, in 1868, a clash ensued between two Black men in Asheville. James Smith, a Republican, attacked Silas, who had voted conservative. Several White members of the community came to the aid of Silas. After the violence ended, Smith was dead and eighteen other African Americans were wounded, along with two White men. Two years later, in Alamance County, members of the Ku Klux Klan hanged Wyatt Outlaw. He was the first African American to serve as town commissioner and constable of Graham and was hanged on the courthouse grounds. John W. Stephens, a state senator from North Carolina and a Republican, was executed in Caswell County, leading to the Kirk-Holden War. In 1898, the tense relationship between the races boiled over. White Democrats attacked the Black-owned newspaper in Wilmington on November 10. As many as sixty African Americans were killed. The Republican mayor, city council and other officials, both White and Black, resigned. The Wilmington coup ushered in severe racial segregation not only in North Carolina but also across the South. There is a North Carolina Highway Historical Marker concerning the riot in Wilmington, along with a marker to Alex Manly, the editor of the Black-owned newspaper. The Cape Fear Museum of Science and History also has exhibits on the 1898 event. There are North Carolina Highway Historical Markers regarding the murder of Stephens at the courthouse in Yanceyville and the Kirk-Holden War in Graham.

PIEDMONT

Sit-Ins, Guilford County

A series of U.S. Supreme Court cases and laws in the late nineteenth century greatly restricted the civil liberties of African Americans. Discontent grew through the first half of the twentieth century. While the laws stated that separate but equal facilities, such as schools, had to be maintained, it seldom worked out that way. African American educational opportunities, transportation and prospects in general were almost always subpar. World War II provided new opportunities, and while many wanted to return to the status quo following the war, the wheels of change were already in motion. Some pivotal events include Rosa Parks and the boycott of the Montgomery bus system, the Little Rock Nine in Arkansas, the U.S. Supreme Court ruling in *Brown v. Board of Education* and the Civil Rights Act of 1957. On February 1, 1960, four college students sat down at a lunch counter for Whites in a Woolworth in Greensboro. They refused to leave until the store closed for the evening. Over the next few days, hundreds arrived to join the Greensboro sit-ins. While not the first sit-ins, these were the most important. Eventually, more than seventy thousand people participated in sit-ins across the United States. The Woolworth eventually served food to the original protesters. There is a North Carolina Highway Historical Marker in Greensboro commemorating the event. The Woolworth has been preserved and is now the International Civil Rights Center and Museum. Part of the original lunch counter is located at the North Carolina Museum of History in Raleigh.

Thomas Day, Caswell County

The birthplace of Thomas Day (circa 1801–circa 1861) is unknown, as it might have been in Virginia or possibly in North Carolina. What is certain about Day is that he was a superb cabinetmaker, quite possibly the finest craftsman in the state prior to 1860. By 1823, he was living with his family in Caswell County. While he was a freedman, he was also a slave owner and had White apprentices in his cabinet shop. There is a North Carolina Highway Historic Marker near his home and shop in Milton, and both the North Carolina Museum of History and the Greensboro History Museum have pieces of Day's furniture on display.

Elizabeth Keckly, Orange County

Born a slave, Elizabeth Keckly purchased her freedom and went on to sew dresses for Mary Todd Lincoln. *From* Behind the Scenes; or, Thirty Years a Slave, and Four Years in the White House.

Born in Virginia, Elizabeth Hobbs Keckly (or Keckley) (circa 1820–1907) lived for a number of years in the Orange County area. Keckly was a seamstress; she purchased her freedom while living in St. Louis and then moved to Washington, D.C., where she made dresses for the wives of Stephen Douglas and Jefferson Davis. Later, she developed a close relationship with Mary Todd Lincoln. In 1868, she published *Behind the Scenes; or, Thirty Years a Slave, and Four Years in the White House.* In Hillsborough, there is a North Carolina Highway Historical Maker concerning her life.

Black Wall Street, Durham County

The Triad region of North Carolina became well known for pivotal moments of struggle and transformation from the late nineteenth and into the twentieth century. These included the development of the Bull City Blues, the key Greensboro sit-ins and the growth of Black Wall Street in Durham. Following the Civil War, Durham became a leader in the tobacco industry. This growth brought in many African Americans and created a strong Black middle class with many Black-owned businesses, including the North Carolina Mutual Life Insurance Company, the nation's largest Black-owned insurance company, along with Mechanics and Farmers Bank, the National Religious Training School and Chautauqua (now North Carolina Central University) and newspapers like the *Durham Reformer* and the *North Carolina*

Mutual. There are many markers in the Durham area to commemorate Black Wall Street and its entrepreneurs, including North Carolina Highway Trail Markers denoting Black Wall Street itself, North Carolina Central University and John Merrick (1859–1919), founder of the North Carolina Mutual Life Insurance Company.

Charlotte Hawkins Brown Museum, Alamance County

Charlotte Hawkins Brown had a passion for educating African American children. *State Archives of North Carolina.*

Born in Henderson County, Charlotte Hawkins Brown (1883–1961) moved to Massachusetts at a young age. After one year of college, she began teaching at a rural school for African American children in Sedalia, North Carolina. When the school closed a year later, Brown decided to open her own school, the Palmer Memorial Institute, named for former president of Wellesley College Alice Freeman Palmer. The school operated from 1902 until the 1970s, with more than one thousand African American students. In 1987, the Charlotte Hawkins Brown State Historic Site opened. The Palmer Memorial Institute Historic District was established in 1988. There is a North Carolina Highway Historical Marker in Sedalia.

Oliver Nestus Freeman Round House and African American Museum, Wilson County

Noted African American stonemason Oliver N. Freeman (1882–1955) built at least thirty-six houses in the Wilson area. The Round House, built in 1946, was one of those homes. Freeman used anything he could find, including stones, bricks, bottles and strings, to construct this unique house. The Oliver Nestus Freeman Round House and African American Museum, which opened in 2001, including the Round House, tells the story of the African American community in the Wilson area.

Hiram R. Revels, Cumberland County

Born in Fayetteville in September 1827 to free parents, Hiram Revels was educated locally before moving to Indiana to finish school. He was ordained as an African Methodist Episcopal Church minister in 1845. He traveled frequently, preaching and educating fellow African Americans. When the Civil War started, he helped recruit two Black regiments in Maryland and then served as a chaplain for a Black regiment. Following the war's conclusion, Revels returned to pastoring churches in Mississippi. In 1868, he was elected as an alderman in Natchez and then elected to the Mississippi Senate. In 1870, he was elected by the state senate to fill an unexpired seat in the U.S. Senate, becoming the first African American senator. After one year, he returned to Mississippi and became president of Alcorn University. He later pastored additional churches and edited a newspaper. One North Carolina Highway Historical Marker concerning Revels is in Lincolnton near a barbershop he operated, and another is near his birthplace in Fayetteville.

George E. Davis, Mecklenburg County

Historically, education in rural North Carolina was always a challenge. It was even more so in the African American communities. George Davis (1862–1959), born in Wilmington and educated at Johnson C. Smith University in Charlotte, spearheaded a project to improve education within North Carolina. He stepped down as a professor in 1921 to implement the Rosenwald School program in the state. The project began in 1917. Julius Rosenwald, president of Sears, Roebuck and Company, set up a fund to organize public schools. By 1932, more than 5,000 schools had been constructed. Davis worked on raising matching funds to build and maintain the schools. There were 813 Rosenwald Schools in North Carolina, more than in any other state. There is a North Carolina Highway Historical Marker to Davis near his home in Charlotte. A few of the schools still survive. The Ware Creek Rosenwald School and Community Center is located in Beaufort County, and the Russell School is in Durham County.

There were hundreds of Rosenwald Schools constructed in North Carolina. These included the Kelford School, Bertie County, circa 1927–28 (*top*); the Rock Hill School, Cabarrus County, circa 1923 (*middle*); and the Wilson Mills School, Johnston County, circa 1926–27 (*bottom*). *State Archives of North Carolina.*

The Black Second

Henry P. Cheatham was the third of four African American U.S. House representatives from the Second Congressional District. *State Archives of North Carolina.*

The Second Congressional District was composed of ten counties: Craven, Jones, Halifax, Northampton, Warren, Edgecombe, Greene, Lenoir, Wayne and Wilson. Due to the large population of African Americans, it was often referred to as the "Black Second." The local population elected four different African Americans to serve in the U.S. Congress between 1874 and 1898.

John A. Hyman (1840–1891) was the first. Born enslaved in Warren County, he had been sold and sent to Alabama. After the Civil War, he made his way back to Warren County. Wyman was a delegate to the 1868 North Carolina Constitutional Convention and served in the North Carolina Senate. In 1874, he became the first African American to serve in the U.S. House, serving one term. There is a North Carolina Highway Historical Marker near his home in Warrenton. James E. O'Hara (1844–1905) was probably born in New York City and grew up in the West Indies. He began working as a schoolteacher in New Bern in 1862 and, in 1866, moved to Goldsboro. O'Hara then lived in Washington, D.C., working as a clerk in the U.S. Treasury Department, but by 1873 he had moved to Halifax County. He served as county commissioner and then, in 1883, was elected to the U.S. House, serving two terms. There is a North Carolina Highway Historical Marker near his home near Enfield. Henry Plummer Cheatham (1857–1935) followed O'Hara. He was born enslaved near Henderson, North Carolina, was freed by the Thirteenth Amendment and received his bachelor's and master's degrees from Shaw University. Cheatham worked in schools in Plymouth. He was the first register of deeds in Vance County and was elected to the U.S. House in 1888, serving until 1893. Later, he was appointed recorder of deeds for the District of Columbia by President William McKinley and then served as superintendent of an orphanage in

George H. White is considered the most notable Black Republican leader of the late nineteenth century. *State Archives of North Carolina.*

Oxford. There is a North Carolina Highway Historical Marker near his grave in Oxford. Finally came George Henry White (1852–1918), considered the most notable Black Republican political leader of the era. White was born free in Columbus County, attended local schools and graduated from Howard University. He taught school in New Bern while reading law and was admitted to the bar in 1879. In the political realm, White served in the North Carolina House, North Carolina Senate and as solicitor in the Second Judicial District. In 1896, White was elected to the U.S. House, serving for two terms. Following those terms, he moved to Washington, D.C, and then to Philadelphia, where he was appointed assistant city solicitor. There are North Carolina Highway Historical Markers near his home in New Bern and in Tarboro.

Further Reading:

Jeffrey J. Crow, Paul Escott and Flora J. Hatley, *A History of African Americans in North Carolina* (2002)

Steve M. Miller and J. Timothy Allen, *Slave Escapes & the Underground Railroad in North Carolina* (2016)

LeRae Sikes Umfleet, *A Day of Blood: The 1898 Wilmington Race Riot* (2020)

AUTHORS, HISTORIANS AND BOOKS

Over the past three hundred years, North Carolina has been fortunate to have produced a host of literary talent and important works. Seemingly countless fiction and nonfiction books have poured forth from the pens of those who have called North Carolina home.

COASTAL

Walter Clark, Halifax County

North Carolina Supreme Court chief justice Walter Clark played an important role in documenting the history of the Tar Heel State. *State Archives of North Carolina.*

Walter Clark (1846–1924) filled many different roles throughout North Carolina history. He was a Confederate veteran, farmer, lawyer, public speaker, historian and chief justice of the North Carolina Supreme Court. While Clark wrote on many aspects of North Carolina history, his greatest contributions came as editor of the *State Records on North Carolina* (sixteen volumes, 1895–1911) and *Histories of the Several Regiments and Battalions from North Carolina in the Great War, 1861–1865* (five volumes, 1901). The latter contains a history of every Confederate regiment from the state, written about a member of that regiment. There is a North Carolina Highway Historical Marker near his home in Airlie, Halifax County.

Harriet Jacobs, Chowan County

Published in 1861 under the pseudonym Linda Brent, *Incidents in the Life of a Slave Girl* is considered an American classic. The author was actually Harriet Jacobs (circa 1813–1897). Born into slavery in Edenton, she escaped and made her way to New York, where she worked as a nanny and with the abolitionist movement. During the Civil War and Reconstruction years, she traveled to Union-controlled areas, helping to establish schools for fugitive and freed slaves. *Incidents in the Life of a Slave Girl* is autobiographical, documenting Jacobs's life as a slave and her struggle for freedom. Edenton has a North Carolina Highway Historical Marker commemorating her life.

Lemuel Sawyer, Camden County

Born in Camden County, Lemuel Sawyer (1777–1852) published a play on Blackbeard the pirate in 1824. This play is believed to be the first play written by a North Carolinian on a North Carolina subject featuring North Carolina characters. Sawyer was a lawyer and served in the General Assembly and the U.S. Congress for a number of terms. In Camden County, there is a North Carolina Highway Historical Marker for him.

James Sprunt, New Hanover County

Best known as a chronicler of history in and around the Cape Fear River region, James Sprunt (1846–1924) was a Scottish immigrant who arrived in North Carolina in 1854. Sprunt served on Confederate blockade runners during the Civil War. After the war, Sprunt engaged in the exportation of cotton and naval stores and served as British vice-consul and Imperial German consul. He was very active in the North Carolina Literary and Historical Association. Among the many books and pamphlets he penned was *Chronicles of the Cape Fear Region* (1914). A North Carolina Highway Historical Marker in Wilmington marks his home. He also owned Orton Plantation and had a community college named for him.

PIEDMONT

Billy Graham, Mecklenburg County

Often referred to as the "Pastor to the Presidents," Billy Graham (1918–2018) was born in Charlotte, where he graduated from local schools. After receiving a degree in theology and another in anthropology, Graham began a radio ministry, served as president of the Northwestern Bible College for four years and then traveled as an evangelist. Graham eventually led more than four hundred crusades in 185 countries and territories. Graham personally removed barriers during the days of segregation, inviting Dr. Martin Luther King Jr. to join him in a sixteen-week revival in New York City. Graham met with twelve different presidents, from Harry S Truman to Barack Obama. He also met with many foreign heads of state, including Queen Elizabeth II. His awards were numerous: Presidential Medal of Freedom, Gospel Music Hall of Fame, knighthood, the Salvation Army's Distinguished Service Medal, Gold Award of the George Washington Carver Memorial Institute, Congressional Gold Medal and many others. Graham was the author of thirty-four books that have sold more than 12 million copies, many of them *New York Times* bestsellers. The Billy Graham Library in Charlotte has a museum devoted to his life and ministry.

Reverend Billy Graham was well known for both his preaching and the numerous books he wrote throughout his ministry. *Iredell County Public Library*.

Maya Angelou

Born in Missouri, Maya Angelou (1928–2014) was an often-published poet, essayist, autobiographer and screen personality. She is best known for her seven autobiographies, the first of which is *I Know Why the Caged Bird Sings* (1969). She was also very active in the civil rights movement, working with Dr. Martin Luther King Jr. and Malcom X. In 1982, she moved to North Carolina, taking a position as the Reynolds Professor of American Studies at Wake Forest University. She passed away in Winston-Salem.

Doris Betts

While a student at the University of North Carolina–Greensboro, Doris Betts (1932–2012) won a contest for her fictional story "Mr. Shawn and Father Scott." The Statesville native later joined the faculty at the University of North Carolina–Chapel Hill and continued writing. Betts penned seven novels and three short fiction collections and was honored with three Sir Walter Raleigh Best Fiction awards, the North Carolina Medal and an Academy Award. She is buried at the Pittsboro Presbyterian Church Cemetery, in Chatham County.

C.C. Crittenden, Wake County

A native of Wake Forest, Charles C. Crittenden (1902–1969) earned a PhD in history from Yale University. He taught history, and from 1935 to 1968, he was head of the North Carolina Historical Commission, later renamed the North Carolina Department of Archives and History. Crittenden's slogan "History for all the people" led to the development of historical highway markers and school materials. He also served as editor of the *North Carolina Historical Review* and wrote, cowrote or edited several other books on North Carolina history. There is a North Carolina Highway Historical Marker for him in Wake Forest, near his boyhood home.

Josephus Daniels, Wake County

From the 1880s until 1948, Josephus Daniels (1862–1948) edited and published the largest newspaper in North Carolina. Daniels was born in Washington and educated at what is now Duke University. He studied law

Maya Angelou, pictured here with Governor Jim Martin at the North Carolina Awards in 1987, is best known for her autobiographies. *State Archives of North Carolina.*

Josephus Daniels edited the largest newspaper in North Carolina and served as secretary of the navy under Woodrow Wilson. *Library of Congress.*

but never practiced, instead purchasing several newspapers. Over time, he became increasingly active in the North Carolina Democratic Party. After gaining control of the Raleigh *News and Observer*, he used the newspaper as the official organ of the Democratic Party in the state. While Daniels advocated through his newspaper for prohibition and women's suffrage, he was decidedly opposed to Catholics and African Americans. President Woodrow Wilson appointed Daniels secretary of the navy from 1913 through 1921, and President Franklin D. Roosevelt appointed him ambassador to Mexico, a post he held from 1933 to 1941. Daniels wrote several books, including a biography of Woodrow Wilson and a five-volume autobiography in which he regretted his stance on white supremacy in the late nineteenth century. There is a North Carolina Highway Historical Marker near his home in Washington, Beaufort County.

Charles W. Chesnutt, Cumberland County

Charles W. Chesnutt (1858–1932) was eight years old when his family moved from Ohio to Fayetteville. He attended Howard School, followed by a teaching job in Charlotte, and then worked as a school principal in Fayetteville. Chesnutt published his first short story in the *Atlantic Monthly* in 1877, making him the first African American to be published in a national publication. In 1883, he moved to New York City and then back to Ohio, where he passed the bar. Chesnutt published two collections of short stories and a biography of Frederick Douglass. There is a North Carolina Highway Historical Marker at the school where he taught in Fayetteville.

Burke Davis

One thing can certainly be said of Burke Davis (1913–2006): he had a varied career. The Durham native wrote both fiction and nonfiction. He was a graduate of the University of North Carolina–Chapel Hill. *Whisper My Name* (1949) was his first novel. Davis wrote many books on the Civil War, including *Gray Fox* (1956), *Jeb Stuart: The Last Cavalier* (1957) and *To Appomattox: Nine April Days, 1865* (1959). He was awarded the North Carolina Award for Literature in 1973, and he was honored by the North Caroliniana Society in 1990.

John Hope Franklin

Originally from Oklahoma, John Hope Franklin (1915–2009) earned a PhD in history from Harvard University. In 1983, he moved to Durham and became the James B. Duke Professor at Duke University. Among his many works are *The Free Negro in North Carolina, 1790–1860* (1943); *From Slavery to Freedom* (1947); and *The Militant South, 1800–1861*. Franklin was awarded several honorary doctorates and, in 2006, received the John W. Kluge Prize for lifetime achievements in the study of humanities. He also served as president of the Organization of American Historians and the Southern Historical Society.

Paul Green, Chatham County

A playwright who wrote about life in North Carolina in the early twentieth century, Paul Green (1894–1981) was born in Buies Creek, near Lillington. A University of North Carolina–Chapel Hill graduate, he is best known for the outdoor drama *The Lost Colony* (1934), which is still performed annually at Fort Raleigh National Historic Site near Manteo. It is the oldest outdoor drama still performed in the United States. Another of his plays, *In Abraham's Bosom* (1926), won the Pulitzer Prize for Drama. There is a North Carolina Highway Historical Marker near his home south of Chapel Hill, and a cabin he used as a writer's retreat is located at the North Carolina Botanical Garden.

O. Henry, Guilford County

William Sydney Porter (1862–1910), better known as O. Henry, was born in Greensboro. He is remembered for his short stories, including "The Gift of the Magi," "The Ransom of Red Chief" and "The Duplicity of Hargraves." O. Henry died in New York City and is interred at Riverside Cemetery, Asheville. There is a Greensboro, North Carolina Highway Historical Marker near a house where he lived and a statue as well.

Hinton R. Helper, Davie County

Born into a slave-owning family near Mocksville, Hilton Helper (1829–1909) went west looking for gold in the early 1850s. Finding little success, he returned to North Carolina, where he wrote *The Land of Gold: Reality Versus Fiction* (1855). This was followed by *The Impending Crisis in the South* (1859), in which he argued that the growth, prosperity and cultural development of the South was being impeded by slavery. The book was popular in antislavery circles, and Helper was forced to flee from the South. Abraham Lincoln appointed Helper as U.S. consul in Buenos Aires. Ironically, Helper disliked and even feared African Americans. There is a North Carolina Highway Historical Marker near the place of his birth near Mocksville.

George Moses Horton, Chatham County

George Moses Horton (1798–circa 1867) taught himself to read. Born into slavery in Northampton County, he worked on a farm in Chatham County, delivering fruit and other crops to the University of North Carolina. Students gave books to Horton, and the wife of a professor worked to improve his grammar. In 1829, a journalist published a book of Horton's poetry, *The Hope of Liberty*. This was the first book by an African American to be published in the South. Two other books followed. Following the Civil War, Horton, now free, moved to Philadelphia, married and wrote Sunday school stories. He eventually moved to Bexley, Liberia, where he disappeared from history. Horton is known as the "Black Bard of North Carolina." There is a North Carolina Highway Historical Marker near Pittsboro, where he lived.

Randall Jarrell, Guilford County

While not a North Carolina native, Randall Jarrell (1914–1965) spent many years teaching in North Carolina universities. He published several volumes of poetry and was considered a gifted poet, children's author, essayist and brilliant critic. There is a North Carolina Highway Historical Marker denoting his grave at the New Garden Friends Cemetery, Greensboro.

Edward A. Johnston, Wake County

Wake County was the birthplace of Edward Johnston (1860–1944). Born a slave, he graduated from Atlanta University and taught school. He returned to North Carolina to become the principal at Washington School in Raleigh. Wanting to fill a gap in historiography, he wrote *A School History of the Negro Race in America* (1891). It was the first Black textbook in the United States. Johnston later moved to New York, practicing law in Harlem. There is North Carolina Highway Historical Marker where his home was located in Raleigh.

William S. Powell

Johnston County native William S. Powell (1919–2015) had a profound impact on the recorded history of North Carolina for well over half a century. Powell taught North Carolina history and then served as curator of the North Carolina Collection at the University of North Carolina–Chapel Hill, where he later became a professor of North Carolina history. He wrote or edited more than six hundred articles and scores of books, including the *North Carolina Gazetteer* (2010), the *Encyclopedia of North Carolina* (2006) and *North Carolina: A History* (1988). Powell is buried at the Church of the Holy Family Columbarium in Chapel Hill.

Reynolds Price

As a child, Reynolds Price (1933–2011) developed a love for the arts. Born in Macon, Price became the James B. Duke Professor of English at Duke University. Price penned thirty-seven volumes, many of them novels about rural people in North Carolina. Price was a finalist for the National Book Awards in 1979 and the Thomas Wolfe Prize in 2007.

Christian Reid, Rowan County

Frances Christine Fisher Tiernan (1846–1920) was born in Salisbury and wrote under the pen name of Christian Reid. She produced more than fifty novels. *Valerie Aylmer*, published in 1870, was her first. Reid's most popular work was *The Land of the Sky* (1876), a book that depicted the Blue Ridge Mountains of Western North Carolina. Later, the Southern Railway adopted the phrase in advertising part of its route. There is a monument to Reid at the Rowan Public Library and a North Carolina Highway Trail Marker in Salisbury. She is buried at Chestnut Hill Cemetery in Salisbury.

Robert Strange, Cumberland County

Lawyer, judge and U.S. senator were just a few of the titles Robert Strange (1796–1854) held in his lifetime. Strange was born in Virginia and, after college, settled in Fayetteville to practice law. In 1839, he published *Eoneguski, or The Cherokee Chief*. The book is considered one of the first novels set in North Carolina and written about a North Carolina native. Strange has a North Carolina Highway Historical Marker in Fayetteville not far from his home and grave.

MOUNTAINS AND FOOTHILLS

Thomas F. Dixon Jr., Cleveland County

Thomas Dixon Jr. (1864–1946) wrote two bestselling books: *The Leopard's Spots: A Romance of the White Man's Burden, 1865–1900* (1902) and *The Clansman: A Historical Romance of the Ku Klux Klan* (1905). Dixon was born in Shelby and was a graduate of Wake Forest College, Johns Hopkins University and the Greensboro Law School. *The Clansman* was adapted as a movie, *The Birth of a Nation*, considered a landmark of film history and one of the most controversial films ever made. There is a North Carolina Highway Historical Marker near Dixon's grave in Shelby.

Wilma Dykeman

Growing up in Buncombe County gave Wilma Dykeman (1920–2006) a unique glimpse of life in Southern Appalachia. After college, she began to write about the area in a series of novels, including *The Tall Woman* (1962), *The Far Family* (1966) and *Return the Innocent Earth* (1973). She was

Wilma Dykeman wrote a great deal about her home in Western North Carolina. *State Archives of North Carolina.*

also a columnist for the *Knoxville News-Sentinel*, lectured around the country and taught college classes. She is buried at the Beaverdam Baptist Church Cemetery in Buncombe County.

John Ehle

Writing both fiction and nonfiction, Asheville native John Ehle (1925–2018) was a diverse writer. A World War II veteran and graduate of the University of North Carolina–Asheville, he penned eleven novels and six nonfiction books. His most regarded work was *The Land Breakers* (1964). Two of his other novels, *The Journey of August King* (1971) and *The Winter People* (1982), were both turned into movies. He is often considered the "father of Appalachian literature." Ehle was inducted into the North Carolina Literary Hall of Fame and received the Thomas Wolfe Memorial Literary Award, the Lillian Smith Book Award and the Mayflower Award.

Thomas Wolfe wrote plays and novels, often drawing inspiration from the western counties of North Carolina. *State Archives of North Carolina.*

Thomas C. Wolfe, Buncombe County

An Asheville stonecutter had an angel in his storefront window, providing inspiration for Thomas Wolfe (1900–1938). The stonecutter was his father. Wolfe studied at the University of North Carolina–Chapel Hill and at Harvard University. He wrote plays and performed while in school and while teaching English at New York University and traveling through Europe. His best-known novel, *Look Homeward, Angel*, was released in 1929 and was highly successful in the United Kingdom and Germany. He wrote several other popular novels. The Asheville boardinghouse where he grew up is now the Thomas Wolfe Memorial State Historic Site. He is buried at Asheville's Riverside Cemetery.

Horace Kephart, Swain County

Our Southern Highlands (1913) is one of the classic books about North Carolina. The author, Horace Kephart (1862–1931), was not native to the area. After working in several libraries, he found his way to the Smoky Mountains. With his friend, photographer George Masa, Kephart lobbied Congress for the establishment of the Great Smoky Mountains National Park. Kephart also worked on the Appalachian Trails through the area. His first book, *Camping and Woodcraft* (1906), was a collection of articles he had written for *Field and Stream. Our Southern Highlands* was part memoir and part a study of lifestyles in Appalachia. In Bryson City, there is a North Carolina Highway Historical Marker about his life, and Mount Kephart in the Great Smoky Mountains National Park is named in his memory.

Carl Sandburg, Henderson County

Winning one Pulitzer is quite a feat. Winning three Pulitzers is amazing. Carl Sandburg (1878–1967) did just that. Two were for his poetry, and one was for his biography of Abraham Lincoln. Born in Illinois, he lived in

Wisconsin and Michigan before moving to Flat Rock, North Carolina, and purchasing Connemara, the home of former Confederate secretary of the treasury Christopher Memminger. Sandburg produced scores of books—histories, novels, children's stories, poetry and an autobiography. President Lyndon B. Johnson, upon Sandburg's death, wrote that he "was more than the voice of America, more than the poet of its strength and genius. He was America." Connemara is now the Carl Sandburg Home National Historic Site. There is a North Carolina Highway Historical Marker in Flat Rock.

Gloria Houston, Avery County

For many writers, life provides some of the best foundations for their work. Born in Avery County, Gloria Houston (1941–2016) drew much inspiration for her award-winning children's books from the lives of her forebears. *My Great Aunt Arizona* (1992) chronicles the life of Arizona Hughes, who taught in local schools for more than fifty years. *The Year of the Perfect Christmas Tree* (1988) tells of a Christmas tradition of bringing home a Christmas tree. Houston won numerous awards for her many books. The Avery County Historical Museum in Newland features information on Houston, and a sculpture in the courtyard of Belk Library at Appalachian State University portrays a child reading *My Great Aunt Arizona.*

Further Reading:

Georgann Eubanks, *Literary Trails of Eastern North Carolina* (2013)
Georgann Eubanks, *Literary Trails of the North Carolina Piedmont* (2010)
Georgann Eubanks and Donna Campbell, *Literary Trails of the North Carolina Mountains* (2007)

ART AND ARTISTS OF NORTH CAROLINA

North Carolina has an incredible history of connection to the arts, through practitioners, performances, exhibitions and schools. There are many fantastic places across the state to experience all of these artistic opportunities, as well as a few places where visitors can jump in, get their hands dirty and create art themselves.

NORTH CAROLINA ARTISTS

There are, of course, numerous artists, working in a wide array of media, who have connections to North Carolina. While they may not have sites or markers devoted to them, their influences and legacies can be seen across the state and farther afield. Some of these important artists are Asheville native Kenneth Noland (1924–2010), the best-known American Color Field painter; Charlotte native Romare Bearden (1911–1988), who worked with cartoons, oils and collages; "folk artist" Minnie Eva Evans (1892–1987), a Pender County native who painted with oils, graphite, wax and crayon; Vollis Simpson (1919–2013), a Lucama native who built whirligigs out of salvaged metal; Ernest E. Barnes Jr. (1938–2009), a Durham native who was known for his unique style of elongated characters and movements; Maud Gatewood (1934–2004), a Yanceyville native who was a teacher, painter and activist; Mabel Pugh (1891–1986), a Morrisville native who worked as a painter, woodblock printmaker and illustrator; Mary Tannahill (1863–1951), a Warren County native who painted, embroidered and produced prints; John Elwood Bundy (1853–1933), a Guilford County native and American Impressionist painter; and John Thomas Biggers (1924–2001), a Gastonia native muralist.

PIEDMONT

North Carolina School of Art, Forsyth County

The first state-supported school in the United States for performing arts opened in Winston-Salem in 1971. There is a North Carolina Highway Historical Marker. The school, a part of the University of North Carolina system, still offers high school, undergraduate and graduate courses.

Seagrove Pottery/Jugtown, Moore/Randolph/Catawba Counties

For more than two centuries, North Carolina has been known for its natural clay deposits. Native Americans made pottery, as did the early Moravian settlers. Many of the British and German settlers settled in the Seagrove area of Randolph County in the eighteenth century. With the establishment

The pottery seen here on the ground next to the kiln did not survive the firing at Jugtown Pottery. *State Archives of North Carolina.*

of better roads and eventually railroads, local potters were able to transport their wares to a larger market. Today, there are scores of potters and studios in the Seagrove area. There are several markers in nearby communities. In nearby Jugtown is a North Carolina Highway Historical Marker on the pottery industry, commemorating the early settlers. Another North Carolina Highway Historical Marker is located near Corinth, in Catawba County. Also located in Jugtown is a North Carolina Highway Historical Marker to Jacques and Juliana Busbee, a couple credited with fostering the modern interest in folk pottery.

North Carolina Museum of Art, Wake County

Originally created by the North Carolina State Art Society in 1924, the North Carolina Museum of Art could be considered one of the premier museums in North Carolina. The museum first opened in downtown Raleigh in 1956. As the collection outgrew that location, a commission in charge of a new site selected a location just west of Raleigh in the 1960s to house the museum. This new site opened in the 1980s. The museum contains works of art by North Carolinians as well as pieces representing artists from around the globe. There are seventy-five works from the Italian Renaissance, Egyptian funerary art, sculptures from ancient Greece and Rome and a Judaic Art Gallery. Also at the museum is one of the most extensive Rodin collections in the United States.

Southeastern Center for Contemporary Art, Forsyth County

Founded in 1956 by James G. Harris, the Southeastern Center for Contemporary Art features the work of contemporary southern artists. There are numerous rotating exhibits highlighting the work of prominent artists such as Barbara Mellin, Jim Moon, Charlie Brouwer, Jessica Singerman and Charles Edward Williams, among others.

MOUNTAINS

Elliott Daingerfield, Watauga County

Considered one of North Carolina's most prolific artists, Elliott Daingerfield moved from Harpers Ferry, West Virginia, to Fayetteville in his youth. He studied art in New York and received recognition for his paintings on religious subjects. Daingerfield died in 1932 and is buried at Cross Creek Cemetery in Fayetteville. His teenage home is located in Heritage Square in Fayetteville. One of his summer homes, Westglow, is located in Blowing Rock, and the site includes a North Carolina Highway Historical Marker. Edgewood Cottage in Blowing Rock, operated by the Blowing Rock Historical Society, was constructed for Daingerfield circa 1890. It is now home to a summer artist-in-residence program and sits adjacent to the Blowing Rock Art and History Museum.

Penland School of Crafts, Mitchell County

The Penland School was founded in the 1920s by Lucy Morgan. She established the school to help local women to learn to weave, giving them an opportunity to sell their wares. Eventually, pottery and basketry were added to the program. Today, the school, which is in the National Register of Historic Places, teaches not only weaving and pottery but also dyeing, glassblowing, printmaking and painting. Near Spruce Pine, there is a North Carolina Highway Historical Marker about the school.

John C. Campbell Folk School, Clay County

Founded in Brasstown in 1925, the John C. Campbell Folk School was created to foster and preserve the folk arts of North Carolina and the Appalachian Mountains. The site itself is listed in the National Register of Historic Places. The school is still active today, offering both weekend and weeklong classes in in both traditional and contemporary arts, including woodcarving, blacksmithing, music, dance, storytelling, nature studies and many more. There is a museum on campus.

Black Mountain College, Buncombe County

Black Mountain College was established in 1933 and operated under the pretext that art was central to the experience of learning. Many of the faculty and students went on to prominence in the art community. Funding issues forced the closure of the school in 1957. There is a North Carolina Highway Historical Marker in Black Mountain, and the Black Mountain College Museum and Arts Center is located in Asheville.

Further Reading:
Allen H. Eaton, *Handicrafts of the Southern Highlands* (1937)
Mary Emma Harris, *The Arts at Black Mountain College* (1987)
Charles Zug III, *Turners and Burners: The Folk Potters of North Carolina* (1986)

PICKERS, STRUMMERS AND CROONERS

HISTORIC MUSICIANS

North Carolinians can be found playing and singing just about every genre of music. More than a home for important musicians, the Tar Heel State is the place where a number of music styles have their roots. Doc Watson developed a specific style of flatpicking. Carl Story is considered the father of bluegrass gospel. Earl Scruggs popularized the three-finger style of banjo picking. John W. Coltrane was a pioneer at the forefront of free jazz. A great place to start exploring the stories of these musical legends and many others is at the North Carolina Music Hall of Fame in Kannapolis. Organized in 1994, the museum has been in Kannapolis since 2009. Some of the inductees and exhibits include opera sensation Victoria Livengood; Grand Ole Opry and Country Music Hall of Fame member Charlie Daniels; jazz pianist and composer Thelonious Monk; Grammy Award winner Donna Fargo; Clyde L. McPhatter, a doo-wop and R&B legend who was the first artist to be inducted into the Rock and Roll Hall of Fame twice; and Nina Simone, the "High Priestess of Soul." There are, of course, many other artists and contributions to the music industry from across the state.

COASTAL

Radio Milestone, Dare County

Reginald Fessenden (1866–1932) is not a household name to many, but his pioneering technological work helped bring voices into numerous households

Reginald Fessenden (*on the right*) is considered the "Father of Voice Radio." *State Archives of North Carolina.*

through the medium of the radio. Born in Canada in 1866, Fessenden spent several months in 1902 and 1903 on Roanoke Island working for the U.S. Weather Bureau. His job was to transmit weather information via radio waves at coastal stations instead of by telegraph lines. There were towers constructed not only on Roanoke Island but also on Cape Hatteras and Cape Henry. In March 1902, he successfully transmitted a 127-word voice message from Cape Hatteras to Roanoke Island. Fessenden held hundreds of patents and is considered the "Father of Voice Radio." A North Carolina Highway Historical Marker, near the boat landing northwest of Manteo, commemorates the event.

Charlie Daniels

Born in Wilmington, Charlie Daniels (1935–2020) was an American music icon who played and recorded in multiple genres, including country, blues, gospel and bluegrass. He is best known for his Grammy Award–winning song about another state, "The Devil Went Down to Georgia." Daniels was a member of the Grand Ole Opry and inducted into the Country

Music Hall of Fame. Many of the songs he wrote were covered by other artists, including Elvis Presley, Kid Rock and Johnny Cash. He was born in Wilmington and spent his early years in North Carolina, graduating from high school in Chatham County. He is buried in Tennessee.

Percy Heath, New Hanover County

Percy Heath (1923–2005) was born in Wilmington but spent his childhood in Philadelphia and later moved to New York. He played violin but switched to stand-up bass and played with a number of 1940s jazz groups. Heath recorded continually, often playing bass with a number of other musicians. Most of his work was with the Modern Jazz Quartet, but he also recorded with Paul Desmond, Dizzy Gillespie and Miles Davis. He died in Southampton, New York.

PIEDMONT

John Coltrane, Guilford County

Considered the greatest jazz saxophonist in the world, John Coltrane (1926–1967) was born in Hamlet and grew up in High Point. In 1943, he moved to Philadelphia and then later to New York City, where he continued studying music and eventually played professionally with the likes of Dizzy Gillespie, Thelonious Monk, Miles Davis and Earl Bostic. During his lifetime, Coltrane was inducted into the Jazz Hall of Fame. Posthumously, he was honored with two Grammys and a Pulitzer Prize and was inducted into the North Carolina Music Hall of Fame in 2009. There is a statue to Coltrane at the High Point City Hall, and the High Point Museum has a display on his life. He is buried in Farmingdale, New York.

Bull City Blues, Durham County

The African American community in Durham gave birth to a distinctive style of music known as the Bull City Blues. Due to the tobacco industry, many people during the Depression migrated to the Durham area to find work. Fulton Allen, from Wadesboro, came to Durham after losing his eyesight. He was known as Blind Boy Fuller and led the blues movement in the area. Other prominent musicians included Reverend Gary Davis, Bull City Red, Richard Trice, Buddy Moss, Blind Blake and Josh White. Blind Boy Fuller and several others traveled to New York City in the 1930s, recording many tracks that were released by several different labels. Bull City Blues differed from the Delta Blues of the Deep South by drawing more inspiration from other sources. Sadly, the location of the grave of Blind Boy Fuller, who died in 1940, has been lost to history. There is a North Carolina Highway Historical Marker about the Bull City Blues in Durham.

Charlie Poole, Rockingham County

The North Carolina Ramblers was a trio formed in the late 1910s with Charlie Poole playing banjo. Poole (1892–1931) was born in Franklinville and, due to an accident, developed a distinctive three-finger style. The North Carolina Ramblers' first hit was "Don't Let Your Deal Go Down Blues," which sold more than 106,000 copies in 1925. He recorded scores of songs before his early death. Poole is buried at Woodland Cemetery, Rockingham County. There is a North Carolina Highway Historical Marker northwest of Eden.

Thelonious Monk, Nash County

Born in Rocky Mount, Thelonious Monk (1917–1982) is the second-most recorded jazz composer in history. Not long after his birth, the family moved to Manhattan, and at six, Monk began taking piano lessons. By the age of seventeen, he was touring and playing jazz, especially at Minton's Playhouse, a Manhattan nightclub. In 1957, he was playing with John Coltrane. Monk was on the cover of *Time* magazine in 1964, an honor afforded to only five other jazz artists. Monk spent the last decade of his life in seclusion, suffering from mental illness. He is buried at Ferncliff Cemetery, Hartsdale, New York. There is a North Carolina Highway Historical Marker marking his birthplace in Rocky Mount.

Jazz great Thelonious Monk, pictured here in October 1968, frequently played with another North Carolina native, John Coltrane. *Library of Congress.*

MOUNTAINS

Nina Simone, Polk County

Born in Tryon, Nina Simone (1933–2003) is considered the High Priestess of Soul. At an early age, she learned to play piano and, through scholarships, attended Allen High School for Girls in Asheville. After being denied admission to the Juilliard School in New York City, she began singing and playing piano in a nightclub in Atlantic City. Eventually, she recorded forty albums, and in 1958, she had a hit with "I Loves You, Porgy." Simone was involved in the civil rights movement, speaking and singing at various marches. She spent many years living overseas, passing away in France. Simone was honored with a Grammy Hall of Fame Award in 2000, received three honorary degrees and, in 2018, was inducted into the Rock and Roll Hall of Fame. There is a statue honoring her in Tryon.

Doc Watson, Watauga County

Arthel Lane "Doc" Watson (1923–2012) might just be the most honored of all North Carolina musicians. He won seven Grammy Awards, plus the Grammy Lifetime Achievement Award. He was also honored with a National Heritage Fellowship by the National Endowment for the Arts in 1988, was inducted into the International Bluegrass Music Hall of Honor in 2000, received a National Medal of Arts in 1997 and was awarded an honorary doctor of music degree from Berklee College of Music in 2010. Watson was born in Watauga County and was blind from an early age. He developed a unique finger style of picking for guitar and frequently traveled across the country, playing at a wide variety of venues and events, including the Newport Folk Festival in 1963. Watson developed a festival in honor of his son, MerleFest, held each year on the campus of Wilkes Community College. There is a statue of Watson in downtown Boone.

Doc Watson won seven Grammys over the course of his long and illustrious music career. *State Archives of North Carolina.*

Carl Story, Caldwell County

Born in Lenoir, singer-songwriter Carl Story (1916–1995) was called the "Father of Bluegrass Gospel Music" by the governor of Oklahoma. He learned to play the fiddle, guitar and banjo and performed with the Lonesome Mountaineers, Bill Monroe and his own group, the Rambling Mountaineers. He played frequently all over the eastern United States. Story passed away in South Carolina. In 2007, he was inducted into the Bluegrass Hall of Fame.

Earl Scruggs, Cleveland County

Earl Scruggs's (1924–2012) list of accomplishments is legendary. The Cleveland County native was a member of Bill Monroe and the Blue Grass Boys before setting out on his own with Lester Flatt and the Foggy Mountain Boys. Scruggs developed his own style of three-finger banjo picking, often referred to as "Scruggs style." His instrumental piece "Foggy Mountain Breakdown" won two Grammys. Flatt and Scruggs recorded "The Ballad of Jed Clampett," the theme song for the 1960s television show *The Beverly Hillbillies*. The song rose to number one on the *Billboard* charts. Eventually, Scruggs recorded fifty albums. He won four Grammys, a Grammy Lifetime Achievement Award and a National Medal of Arts. He was inducted into the International Bluegrass Hall of Fame and the Country Music Hall of Fame, and he has a star on the Hollywood Walk of Fame. The Earl Scruggs Center in Shelby opened in 2014 and focuses on the life of Scruggs, along with the music and culture of the South.

Lulu Belle and Scotty, Avery County

They were the "Sweethearts of Country Music." Lulu Belle (Myrtle Cooper, Boone, 1913–1999) and Scott Wiseman (Ingalls, 1909–1981) were some of the most popular entertainers in the United States in the 1930s. While they were born only a county apart, they did not meet until performing together on the *National Barn Dance* on WLS in Chicago in 1934. Their hit "Have I Told You Lately that I Love You" was a national success, and not just in country music. This song was also recorded by Bing Crosby and the Andrews Sisters, Elvis Presley, Gene Autry, Red Foley, Little Jimmy Dickens, Ringo Starr and

Above: Carl Story, *second from the left*, is considered the "Father of Bluegrass Gospel." *Caldwell Heritage Museum.*

Left: Although they were both born in North Carolina, Lulu Belle and Scotty did not meet until they were performing on WLS in Chicago. *Avery County Historical Museum.*

Willie Nelson. They were the first country music stars to venture into feature motion pictures, starring in *Village Barn Dance* (1940), *Shine On, Harvest Moon* (1938), *Sing, Neighbor, Sing* (1944) and *The National Barn Dance* (1944). Lulu Belle was named the Favorite Female Radio Star in the United States in 1938. They semi-retired to Avery County in 1958. Scotty was inducted into the Country Music Hall of Fame in 1970 and the Nashville Songwriters Hall of Fame in 1971, and together they were inducted into the North Carolina Music Hall of Fame and the Blue Ridge Music Hall of Fame. They are buried at Pine Grove United Methodist Church in Avery County, and the Avery County History Museum in Newland has an outstanding exhibit on their lives.

Further Reading:

Elizabeth Carlson and Paul Brown, *North Carolina String Music Masters: Old-Time and Bluegrass Legends* (2016)

Fred C. Fussell and Steve Kruger, *Blue Ridge Music Trails of North Carolina: A Guide to Music Sites, Artists, and Traditions of the Mountains and Foothills* (2018)

David Menconi, *Step It Up and Go: The Story of North Carolina Popular Music, from Blind Boy Fuller and Doc Watson to Nina Simone and Superchunk* (2020)

LIGHTS, CAMERA, ACTION!

ACTORS, ACTRESSES AND LOCATIONS

Andy Griffith, Ava Gardner, Cecil B. DeMille and Soupy Sales are just some of the most iconic Hollywood personalities who have North Carolina roots. Not only does North Carolina have a few famous screen favorites, but the state has also been the site of numerous film and television productions.

AVA GARDNER MUSEUM, JOHNSTON COUNTY

Often considered the most beautiful woman to ever step in front of a camera, Ava Gardner was born in Grabtown, near Smithfield, North Carolina, in 1922. Growing up, she also lived in Newport News and Rock Ridge, near Wilson, North Carolina. A publicity photograph taken while in New York City led to an interview with an MGM scout. She was hired in 1941 and moved to Hollywood. Over the next forty years, Gardner starred in scores of films alongside some of the industry's leading men, including Gregory Peck, Clark Gable, Humphrey Bogart, Errol Flynn, Robert Taylor, Burt Lancaster and Charlton Heston. She was nominated for a 1953 Academy Award for *Mogambo* but lost to Audrey Hepburn. She was also nominated for a BAFTA Award and a Golden Globe. Later in life, she lived in England and Spain. She passed away in January 1990 and is buried at the Sunset Memorial Park in Smithfield. In 1996, the Ava Gardner Museum in Smithfield was incorporated. The museum has posters, dresses she owned and wore in films and even some of the books from her own collection.

ANDY GRIFFITH MUSEUM, SURRY COUNTY

Born in 1926 in Mount Airy, Andy Griffith was one of the nation's most beloved television entertainers and one of North Carolina's best-known sons. Griffith graduated with a degree in music from the University of North Carolina–Chapel Hill and went on to teach music and drama in Goldsboro. On the side, Griffith began to write and record. Colonial Records recorded and released "What It Was, Was Football," which reached number nine on the charts in 1954. By 1955, Griffith was breaking into acting, starring in *No Time for Sergeants* in 1955 and *A Face in the Crowd* in 1957. Beginning in 1960, Griffith starred as Sheriff Andy Taylor in *The Andy Griffith Show*. The show ended in 1968 and is probably Griffith's best-known work. Most of Griffith's screen work was for television, with the series *Matlock* being his second-best known. However, he also made appearances on *The Mod Squad*, *Hawaii Five-O*, *The Bionic Woman*, *Fantasy Island* and *Dawson's Creek*. Griffith passed away at his home in Manteo, Roanoke Island, in July 2012. Mount Airy has unofficially become Mayberry, the fictional town in *The Andy Griffith Show*, although the show was filmed in Hollywood. Visitors can stop by Floyd's Barbershop or eat at the Snappy Lunch. The Andy Griffith Museum opened in 2009 and displays clothing that he and others wore on various shows, some of Griffith's records and mockups of the jail. The Mount Airy Regional Museum also has an exhibit on Griffith's life.

Andy Griffith was one of the most beloved actors from North Carolina. *State Archives of North Carolina.*

DEMILLE FAMILY, BEAUFORT COUNTY

It would be hard to overstate the importance of the DeMille family in American history. Henry C. DeMille was born in Washington, Beaufort County, in 1853. Following the Civil War, he lived with his grandfather and then attended Columbia University, later teaching school. Beginning in 1886, he wrote some of the most popular plays in United States history, including *Lord Chumley*, *The Charity Ball* and *The Lost Paradise*. One of DeMille's sons was William C. DeMille, a noted playwright and silent film director, who was born in Beaufort County. Another son was Cecil B. DeMille, the founder of the Hollywood motion picture industry. *The Squaw Man*, his first film, is considered the first feature film shot in Hollywood. Among his pivotal productions were *The Ten Commandments*, *The King of Kings* and *The Greatest Show on Earth*. There is a Washington North Carolina Highway Historical Marker to the family.

OTHER ACTORS AND ACTRESSES

There are many actors and television personalities who have ties to North Carolina but are not memorialized in any way. These include Soupy Sales (1926–2009), a comedian born in Franklinton and best known for *Lunch with Soupy Sales* and his trademark pie-in-the face routine at the end of each show. Murray Hamilton (1923–1986) was born in Washington and appeared in films such as *Anatomy of a Murder*, *The Amityville Horror* and *Jaws*. Kathryn Grayson (1922–2010) was born in Winston-Salem and starred in *Kiss Me Kate* and *Show Boat*. Collin Wilcox (1935–2009) grew up in Highlands, starred in *To Kill a Mockingbird* and appeared in several episodes of various television series, including *The Twilight Zone*, *Gunsmoke* and *Columbo*. Edith Fellows (1923–2011), who grew up in Charlotte, was acting as early as 1929, when she starred in Charley Chase's *Movie Knight*. Fellows was in scores of other films. Anita Morris (1943–1994) was born in Durham and started out on Broadway, acting in *Jesus Christ Superstar*, *Seesaw* and *Nine*. On film, she gave numerous big screen and television performances, including in *Bloodhounds of Broadway* and *The Hotel New Hampshire*. On television, Morris was in episodes of *Down and Out in Beverly Hills*, *Cheers*, *Miami Vice*, *Matlock* and *Murder, She Wrote*. Elvia Allman (1904–1992) was born in Enochville and is best known for appearing in episodes of *The Beverly Hillbillies*, *Petticoat Junction* and *I Love Lucy*. Jackie "Moms" Mabley (1894–1975) was a comedian and actress born in Brevard. She performed in traveling vaudeville shows and films and later appeared

Charles Kuralt spent many years behind the anchor desk. *State Archives of North Carolina.*

on shows like *The Smothers Brothers Comedy Hour*, *The Ed Sullivan Show* and *The Pearl Bailey Show*. Howard Cosell (1918–1995) was born in Winston-Salem, attended school in New York, earned a law degree, served in World War II and became one of the all-time great sportscasters. David Brinkley (1920–2003) hailed from Wilmington. He attended the University of North Carolina–Chapel Hill and, from 1943 until his retirement in 1997, worked as a television journalist. Charles Kuralt (1934–1997) was also born in Wilmington and was an American journalist. He also attended the University of North Carolina–Chapel Hill and served in a variety of posts with CBS.

FILMMAKING IN NORTH CAROLINA

For filmmakers, North Carolina is an attractive location. There are beaches, mountains, sandhills and longleaf forests. One estimate places the number of movies shot in North Carolina over the past century at three thousand. It is not possible to list all of those here, but some of the more popular movies filmed here, in whole or part, include *Bull Durham*, *Nights in Rodanthe*, *The Winter People* and *Cape Fear*. There have been several places in North Carolina that have served as important backdrops for many different films. Some of these are popular destinations for fans who want to see where their favorite movies were created.

The Biltmore mansion and estate grounds have served as locations in numerous films, including ones as disparate as *The Swan*, with Grace Kelly, and *Hannibal*, starring Anthony Hopkins and Gary Oldman. The Biltmore often hosts traveling exhibitions of costumes and props from period films.

Lake Lure was the site for filming much of *Dirty Dancing*, standing in for the fictional Kellerman's Resort in Upstate New York. The popular movie, which stars Patrick Swayze and Jennifer Grey, still draws fans to the lake.

Wilmington was the filming site for segments of *Matlock*, a courtroom drama series starring Andy Griffith as an affable but brilliant lawyer.

Salisbury, Charlotte and Wadesboro were all used as locations for the award-winning film *The Color Purple*, based on Alice Walker's novel, directed by Steven Spielberg and starring Danny Glover, Whoopi Goldberg and Oprah Winfrey.

Charlotte and Wilkesboro were some of the filming locations used for the stock car racing drama *Days of Thunder*, starring Tom Cruise, Nicole Kidman and Robert Duvall.

Duke University, the James Adams Buchanan House in Durham and Raleigh were all used as locations in the 1990 film adaptation of Margaret Atwood's dystopian novel *The Handmaid's Tale*, starring Natasha Richardson, Faye Dunaway and Robert Duvall.

Wrightsville Beach and Kure Beach provided locations for the 1991 thriller *Sleeping with the Enemy*, in which Julia Roberts plays a woman who fakes her own death to escape her abusive husband, played by Patrick Bergin.

Chimney Rock, Linville Falls, Hickory Nut Falls and the Biltmore Estate were all used in the filming of 1992's *The Last of the Mohicans*, based on James Fenimore Cooper's classic novel. Starring award-winning actor Daniel Day-Lewis as the iconic Hawkeye, the film includes sweeping vistas of the North Carolina mountains, standing in for the Catskills of Cooper's novel.

Grandfather Mountain and the Biltmore Estate were some of the many locations used in filming the Academy Award–winning *Forrest Gump*, starring Tom Hanks. Grandfather Mountain now has a sign for "Forrest Gump Curve" to mark one of the locations where the character is depicted running across America.

Fontana Lake, Robbinsville and Charlotte were all used in 1994's *Nell*, with Jodie Foster, Liam Neeson and Natasha Richardson as leads in a film that is actually set in North Carolina, telling the story of a remarkable but socially isolated young woman.

The Cone Manor House, in Blowing Rock, provided the backdrop for the nursing home scenes in *The Green Mile*, a 1999 film starring Tom Hanks and based on Stephen King's short story.

Wrightsville Beach, Burgaw, Faison and Wilmington were all locations used in the *Divine Secrets of the Ya-Ya Sisterhood*, with Sandra Bullock, Ellen Burstyn and Fionnula Flanagan in lead roles.

Charlotte and Rockingham, specifically their speedways, provided locations for the Will Ferrell comedy *Talladega Nights: The Ballad of Ricky Bobby*, which largely draws on Tom Cruise's *Days of Thunder*, also filmed in the state.

Henry River Mill Village in Hildebran, along with other locations in Shelby, Pisgah National Forest, Asheville, Concord and Charlotte, provided the locations for the 2012 film adaptation of Suzanne Collins's best-selling novel *The Hunger Games*, starring Jennifer Lawrence, Josh Hutcherson and Woody Harrelson. The village site was altered to resemble the story's District 12.

Kenansville, Wilmington, Rose Hill, Oak Island, Cary and Currie were all used as locations for filming Marvel's *Iron Man 3*, starring Robert Downey Jr., Gwyneth Paltrow and Guy Pearce.

Wilmington and Southport were employed extensively as locations for the 2013 romantic film *Safe Haven*, based on Nicholas Sparks's best-selling novel. Film fans can take a tour of the sites used for the film.

Wilmington and Kure Beach provided the earthly locations for 1999's *Muppets from Space*, in which Kermit, Miss Piggy and a host of Muppets and guest stars help Gonzo the Great reconnect with his family.

Further Reading:

Connie Nelson and Floyd Harris, *Film Junkie's Guide to North Carolina* (2004)

"START YOUR ENGINES!"

NASCAR

Stock car racing, which really had its beginnings in North Carolina, became the official state sport in 2011. The history is almost a century older. Local moonshine manufacturers would rebuild the engines in their cars to make them faster as they attempted to outrun law enforcement while transporting their product to markets in Charlotte, Atlanta and other major cities in the region. Dirt tracks soon sprang up across the state, often at county fairs, where local drivers could race against one another. Stock car racing, as it is known today, began after World War II when "Big Bill" France formed the National Association for Stock Car Racing in 1947. Of the fifty-two NASCAR races held the next year, thirty of them were in North Carolina, at places like North Wilkesboro, Lexington, Elkin and Charlotte. The first Strictly Stock Division race was held in Charlotte in June 1949. A North Carolina Highway Historical Marker is near the site off Little Rock Road. In addition to those mentioned here, many other race teams have museums in their shops.

NASCAR HALL OF FAME, MECKLENBURG COUNTY

While NASCAR might have been birthed in Florida on the beaches of Daytona, North Carolina has become its home. Many teams and drivers make their homes in the Piedmont section of the state. In 2010, the NASCAR Hall of Fame opened in Charlotte. There are numerous displays that include cars, a car hauler, racing suits, trophies and memorabilia spanning the various eras of NASCAR history. Parts of the galleries change every year with the announcements and inductions of drivers, owners and crew members into the Hall of Fame.

WILKES COUNTY HERITAGE MUSEUM, WILKES COUNTY

One of the most famous figures in NASCAR history is Junior Johnson. Winning fifty NASCAR races in the 1950s and 1960s, including the 1960 Daytona 500, Johnson went on to become a team owner, winning the NASCAR championship with two different drivers. The Wilkes County Heritage Museum has displays about Johnson's racing and team ownership careers, as well as one of his original cars, along with numerous other pieces of racing history. Down the road is the North Wilkesboro Speedway. Races were held there often from 1949 until its closure in 1996. There is a North Carolina Highway Historical Marker on Speedway Road.

RICHARD PETTY MUSEUM, RANDOLPH COUNTY

The Petty family has a long history of racing in North Carolina. Lee Petty, from Randolph County, won fifty-four NASCAR races and was three times the Grand National Driving Champion. His son, Richard Petty, with two hundred wins, is the all-time-winningest NASCAR driver. The museum, located at the former shop in Level Cross, is packed full of racing memorabilia. There are race cars that won numerous races, including the Daytona 500. Some of Richard Petty's personal collections are presented as well.

OCCOONEECHEE SPEEDWAY, ORANGE COUNTY

In the nineteenth century, the area that became the Occooneechee Speedway was property owned by Julian S. Carr and was used to race horses. In the 1940s, Bill France constructed a 9/10-mile dirt track. From 1949 to 1968, the dirt track Occooneechee Speedway was one of the fastest on the NASCAR circuit. Louise Smith became the first female NASCAR driver to race at the track in 1949. Some of the most popular drivers of all time—such as Junior Johnson, Ned Jarrett and Fireball Roberts—raced here. Richard Petty won the final race here on September 15, 1968. Today, the track is a walking trail open to the public.

The Charlotte Motor Speedway is one of the most featured tracks on the NASCAR circuit. *State Archives of North Carolina.*

Famed NASCAR legend and North Carolina native Richard Petty at Daytona Speedway. *State Archives of North Carolina.*

RCR MUSEUM, DAVIDSON COUNTY

There are a number of iconic drivers with roots in North Carolina throughout the history of NASCAR. One such driver was Dale Earnhardt. A seven-time cup winner, Earnhardt worked with Richard Childress Racing before his tragic death in the final lap of the Daytona 500 in 2001. From 1984 to 2001, Earnhardt drove for Richard Childress Racing, and much of the work on the cars took place in the shop that is now the RCR Museum in Welcome. There are many iconic Earnhardt cars at the RCR Museum, including the 1998 Daytona 500–winning car and the 1995 Brickyard 400–winning car. There are also cars belonging to Kevin Harvick, Dale Earnhardt Jr., Austin Dillon and Ricky Rudd. There are numerous trophies, fire suits and other pieces of the racing past on display.

North Carolina Auto Racing Hall of Fame, Iredell County

With numerous race teams located nearby, Mooresville is the de facto epicenter of NASCAR. It is also the home to the North Carolina Auto Racing Fall of Fame. The idea for the museum originated with the elected officials in Mooresville, the chamber of commerce and Don Miller, president of Penske Racing South. The first hall of fame inductee in 1997 was "The King," Richard Petty. Others have included Junior Johnson, Lee Petty, Ned Jarrett, Dale Earnhardt and Richard Childress. The museum has an impressive collection of racecars, from a 1932 Ford to drag cars and NASCAR cars, with plenty of racing memorabilia.

Further Reading:

Marc P. Singer and Ryan L. Sumner, *Auto Racing in Charlotte and the Carolina Piedmont* (2003)

Deb Williams and Darrell Waltrip, *Charlotte Motor Speedway: From Granite to Gold* (2013)

Perry Allen Wood, *Silent Speedways of the Carolinas: The Grand National Histories of 29 Former Tracks* (2007)

DIG IN!

HISTORIC MINING SITES

While it might seem strange that North Carolina was once the mining capital of the United States, there is a long, deep Tar Heel history of digging into the earth for its rich resources. Native Americans mined mica from the western counties during the mid-Woodland Hopewell era. Some of this mica has been found in mounds in Ohio. Later, the Spanish arrived, exploring some of these mines, looking for gold and silver. Many different types of mining have occurred in North Carolina. There are copper mines in Ashe County; coal mines in Lee, Moore and Chatham Counties; and iron mines across the state, from Avery County to Beaufort County. Two of the treasures from the earth that have truly pushed North Carolina to the forefront of history are gold and mica.

REED GOLD MINE STATE HISTORIC SITE, CABARRUS COUNTY

On a Sunday morning in 1799, twelve-year-old Conrad Reed went fishing and came home with a seventeen-pound rock he found in Little Meadow Creek, Cabarrus County. The rock served as a doorstop for three years before his father, John Reed, took it to Fayetteville, learned that it was gold and sold it. Word of the discovery soon got out, and the first gold rush in the United States was underway. The rush went on until 1829, when gold was discovered in the mountains of Georgia. This new discovery drew some attention from

Bill Jenkins mined in the Gold Hill region, circa 1857. *State Archives of North Carolina.*

North Carolina, but the state led the nation in gold production until 1847 and gold mining continued into the twentieth century. The focus was not just on Cabarrus County but also on the mountain counties of McDowell and Burke, all throughout the Piedmont counties. Men, women, children and enslaved people were all involved in the pursuit. For some, mining was a full-time occupation, while others headed to a creek to pan for gold once their farming chores were completed. The Reed Gold Mine State Historic Site in Midlands has exhibits on mining in the area, along with tours of a mining shaft. There are numerous North Carolina State Historical Markers across the piedmont section of North Carolina that tell the story of old mines. These include the Barringer Mine, Stanley County; Gold Mines, Nash County; Gold Mines, Mecklenburg County; and the Gold Hill Mining District, Rowan County.

BECHTLER MINT SITE HISTORIC PARK, RUTHERFORD COUNTY

For years, gold was sent to the U.S. Mint in Philadelphia for processing or used locally for commerce. In 1832, Christopher Bechtler constructed his own mint, producing the United States' first $1.00 gold coin. He also minted $2.50 and $5.00 pieces. Over the next twenty years, the mint produced $2.24 million in gold coins. The Bechtler Mint Site Historic Park in Rutherfordton is the location of the original mint.

THE MINT MUSEUM, MECKLENBURG COUNTY

With so much gold being mined in North Carolina, local people began petitioning Congress for a branch of the U.S. Mint. In 1835, Congress finally agreed, and the U.S. Mint in Charlotte opened in 1837, producing $2.50 and $5.00 pieces. Over the course of nine years, $5 million worth of gold coins was produced. The mint closed at the beginning of the Civil War, although the building was used to store Confederate gold in April 1865. Following the war, no other coins were minted, although there was still an assayer's office located in the building. The building was moved in the 1930s and opened as a museum in 1936.

THE MUSEUM OF NORTH CAROLINA MINERALS, MITCHELL COUNTY

Across the counties of Avery, Mitchell and Yancey, there are 247 different varieties of minerals and rocks in the ground. These include quartz, emeralds, feldspar, graphite, beryl, aquamarine, garnets, nickel, rubies, sapphires and mica. This area is known as the Spruce Pine Mining District. Over the centuries, mica has had multiple uses. At first, it was used for windows in homes, churches and stores and then as shades for lights and as furnace viewing glass. When Thomas Edison built the electric motor in 1878, he is rumored to have used mica from the Spruce Pine area in his capacitors. In 1909, the Tar Heel Mica Company was founded. By 1923, the *Winston-Salem Journal* was reporting that this company was the second-largest mica company in the world. The Great Depression hit the mica industry hard, and it became cheaper to import mica from India than to mine it domestically. The beginning of World War II changed this situation, and domestic mica production soared. Mica was used in electronics of all kinds, including aircraft, radio and radar equipment. A 1942 map of the Spruce Pine Mining District shows 375 mines in just those three counties. The Meadow Mine in Avery County was the largest mica mine in the United States. There were mica mines in Jackson, Haywood and other mountain counties as well.

The Museum of North Carolina Minerals, in Spruce Pine, is located right off the Blue Ridge Parkway and opened in 1955. The museum was a joint venture between the State of North Carolina and the National Park Service. The museum features displays on mica but also on many of the other minerals and rocks mined in North Carolina. There is also a North Carolina Highways Historical Marker on the grounds.

There are a few other mineral museums of note in North Carolina. These include the Gem and Mineral Museum of Franklin, located in an old jail, and the Mineral and Lapidary Museum of Henderson County in Hendersonville.

Further Reading:

Richard Knapp and Brent Glass, *Gold Mining in North Carolina* (1999)
Robert Schabilton, *Down the Crabtree* (2009)

ALL ABOARD!

NORTH CAROLINA'S RAIL HISTORY

Even today, trains continue to capture many people's imaginations. North Carolina's railroading history stretches back to the 1830s. When the 161-mile-long Wilmington and Weldon was finished in 1840, it was the longest railroad line in the world. The state government was a major financial backer of various railroad projects. During the Civil War years, North Carolina railroads became major carriers of troops and supplies, not only from the state but also through the state. After the war, many of the lines were quickly repaired, and new lines soon sprang up. In 1920, North Carolina had 5,522 miles of railroad. However, the Great Depression and loss of passenger service due to the spread of automobiles and good roads led to a reduction of lines. Many were abandoned, while others were absorbed by larger railroad companies. By the turn of the twenty-first century, only a little more than 3,500 miles of track remained in North Carolina.

There are numerous North Carolina Highway Historical Markers across the state marking important milestones in railroad history. A few of those include a marker in Alamance County close to where the first public meeting concerning a railroad took place in 1828; an experimental railroad in Raleigh, used to help transport granite for the state capitol in 1833; the first railroad in the state that ran from Petersburg, Virginia, into Northampton County in 1833; and the Saluda Grade, in Saluda, the steepest standard-gauge track in the United States, which opened in 1878. There are also numerous old depots across the state that are simply interesting roadside places to see and photograph.

COASTAL

Wilmington Railroad Museum, New Hanover County

Wilmington has a grand railroading history. The city was the terminus for the Wilmington and Raleigh (later Weldon) Railroad, the longest railroad in the world when completed in 1840. That line became an official part of the Atlantic Coast Line Railroad in 1900. The company headquarters for the Atlantic Coast Line were located in Wilmington. In 1960, company offices were moved to Jacksonville, Florida, a blow to the local economy. The line eventually became CSX. The Wilmington Railroad Museum was created in 1979 and in 2007 moved into the former ACL freight warehouse. Not only are there numerous exhibits, but the museum also has an original steam locomotive, boxcar and caboose. In 2011, model railroad enthusiasts from the museum broke the Guinness World Record for the world's longest model railroad.

PIEDMONT

Kernersville Depot, Forsyth County

The town of Kernersville was two years old when the Northwestern North Carolina Railroad arrived in 1873. A depot was built that served as a hub of commerce until 1940, when a new depot was built across the street. The old depot served as a warehouse. Eventually, the new depot was demolished, and the old Kernersville Depot was moved and restored.

North Carolina Railway Museum, Wake County

Durham's tobacco industry was so large around the turn of the twentieth century that six different railroads were needed to serve the area. One of those was the Durham and South Carolina Railroad. From Durham, this line ran south, eventually into Harnett County. The line was acquired by Norfolk Southern in 1957 and Southern Railway in 1982. Parts of the line were dismantled in 1985. The East Carolina Chapter of the National Railway Historical Society acquired the surviving parts of the line near Bonsal and opened the New Hope Valley Railway. The museum has

The depot in Raleigh was a hubbub of activity in the heyday of the railroad. The building survives, but the train no longer runs. *State Archives of North Carolina.*

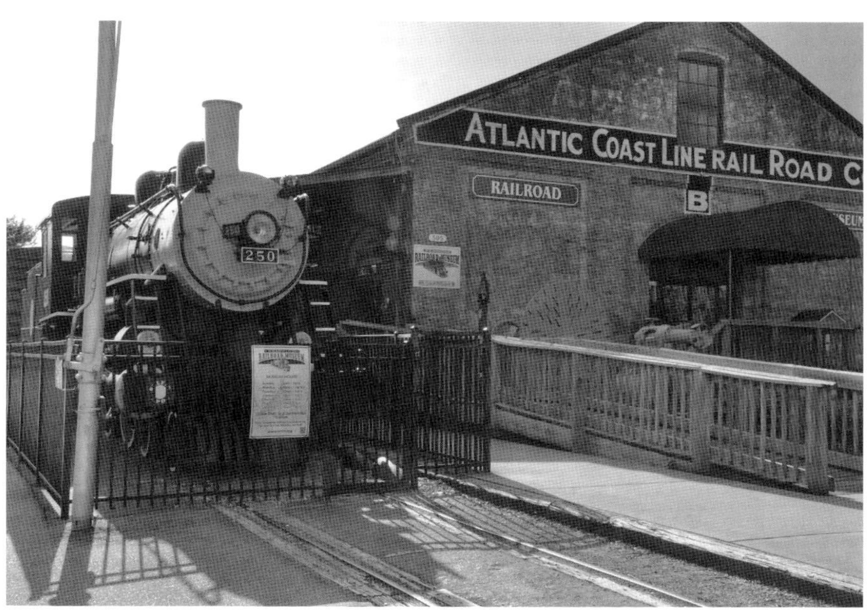

Wilmington's Railroad Museum is located in an old Atlantic Coast Line freight warehouse. *Author's collection.*

several pieces of rolling stock, including a mail car, box cars, a caboose and several engines. On weekends, excursion rides on four miles of track are available.

North Carolina Museum of Transportation, Rowan County

Spencer Shops was the Southern Railway's largest repair shop in the Southeast. This section of the railroad stretched more than six hundred miles between Washington, D.C., and Atlanta. Eventually, the Southern Railway served thirteen states with more than eight thousand miles of track. The repair and maintenance facility at Spencer opened in 1896. Eventually, Spencer Shops included a thirty-seven-stall roundhouse (the second on the property); the back shop, which at ninety thousand square feet was once the largest industrial building in North Carolina (constructed in 1905); and a flue shop, storehouse and master mechanic's office. Every engine was brought into the roundhouse for maintenance, and some engines would be moved through the back shop for a complete overhaul,

The North Carolina Museum of Transportation in Spencer has one of the best collections of rolling stock in the South. *Author's collection.*

which only took days. With the arrival of diesel locomotives, there was less need for a steam locomotive repair shop. The facilities were closed in the 1960s. In 1977, the Southern Railway deeded the property to the State of North Carolina for a transportation museum. The first exhibit opened in 1983. Over the years, many of the buildings have been restored and new exhibits added. These include the back shop and the Bob Julian Roundhouse. The 1898 depot from the community of Barber was moved to the site and opened in 1996. Today, the museum has an impressive collection of steam and diesel locomotives, along with passenger cars, box cars, cabooses, a U.S. Mail car and a World War II hospital railcar. The site offers train excursions. Work on repairing various pieces of locomotive history takes place in the roundhouse. There are also other exhibits on North Carolina's automotive and aerospace history, including a replica of the Wright Flyer and displays on the Carolina-based Piedmont Airlines.

Southeastern Narrow Gauge and Shortline Museum, Catawba County

In 1882, the Chester and Lenoir Railroad arrived in Newton. This narrow-gauge line was converted to standard gauge in 1902 when it was acquired by the Carolina and Northwestern, a subsidiary of the Southern Railroad. There were plans to demolish the 1924 Newton Depot in the 1990s. The Newton Depot Authority was created, which acquired the depot, moved it a half mile to its current location and restored the building. It now serves as the Southeastern Narrow Gauge and Shortline Museum. Located nearby is the Alexander Railroad Pavilion, which has an impressive collection of narrow- and standard-gauge rolling stock, including the circa 1875 Carolina and Northwestern wooden boxcar, the ET&WNC boxcar no. 434 and the Virginia-Carolina no. 50, a 1922 standard-gauge Alco 2-6-0.

Hamlet Depot and Museums, Richmond County

At one time, Hamlet, North Carolina, contained the largest rolling stock classification yard in the world. Trains still run through Hamlet today, and the area has a fine collection of railroad museums. The town was founded in 1897 and served as a division headquarters for the Seaboard Airline Railroad. Nearly thirty passenger trains per day often passed through the town. Around the turn of the century, a depot was constructed in the Queen Anne style. The building has been restored and is one of the museums in a complex. Nearby is the Tornado Building, which contains a replica of the "Tornado," possibly the first steam locomotive to enter Raleigh in 1840. Also in town is the National Railroad Museum and Hall of Fame, which opened in 1976 and is located beside the Hamlet Depot.

Union Station Railroad Museum, Moore County

Chartered in 1892, the Aberdeen and Rockfish Railroad Company was built to move lumber and turpentine. The line continued to expand over time and remains one of the most successful shortlines in the United States. The depot in Aberdeen, Union Station, was constructed in 1900. There is a restored caboose nearby.

MOUNTAINS

Avery County Historical Museum, Avery County

While not in its original location, the last remaining Linville River Railway Depot can be visited at the Avery County Historical Museum. The depot, which also served the East Tennessee and Western North Carolina Railroad, was constructed in 1917. With chestnut bark siding and window boxes for flowers, it was the nicest depot on the line. After the flood of 1940, the Linville Depot served as a convenience store and then as a residence. The depot was moved for a third time to the museum grounds in 2007 and restored. Beside the depot is the ET&WNC Caboose 505, the only remaining caboose from the fabled Tweetsie line. It has also been restored and is open for tours. The Avery County Historical Museum is located in the 1913 Avery County jail in Newland.

Tweetsie Railroad, Watauga County

While it does not travel on an original section of railroad, Engine No. 12, a 4-6-0 Baldwin narrow-gauge locomotive, is original to the area. Constructed in 1917, the engine hauled lumber and iron ore from the area into east

Tennessee from 1919 to 1940. The engine was placed into the National Register of Historic Places in 1992 and, since 1957, has been hauling delighted guests around the Tweetsie Wild West Theme Park.

Great Smoky Mountains Railroad, Swain County

It usually took many years and much labor to build railroads in the mountain areas of Western North Carolina. After a line was surveyed and the property acquired, the new line often had to be blasted out of the side of a mountain. There were tunnels, fills, trestles and much grading work needed to traverse the mountain, with much of the work being provided by Black convicts from the state prison. The Murphy Branch of the Western North Carolina Railroad headed west from Asheville in 1880. Timber was a chief product of the line, eventually owned by the Southern Railway, while passengers and mixed freight helped keep the line in business. With the decline of the lumber industry and the loss of passenger service, it was no longer feasible to keep the line. It was acquired by the State of North Carolina, and in 1988, the Great Smoky Mountains Railway opened, running excursion trains into the Nantahala Gorge. About two hundred thousand people per year take the forty-plus-mile trip. Nearby is the Smoky Mountain Train museum, with a large model train layout.

Further Reading:

Burke Davis, *The Southern Railway: Road of Innovators* (1985)

Larry K. Neal Jr. and Jim Wrinn, *Southern Railway's Historic Spencer Shops* (2011)

John R. Waite, *The Blue Ridge Stemwinder* (2003)

ON THE ROAD

HISTORIC MOTORWAYS

When settlers from Europe first arrived, they found an area crisscrossed by roads and trails created by humans and animals. Native American tribes moved frequently, warring or trading with other tribes. Settlers sometimes improved these existing trails or those made by buffalo and other wildlife. Roads were rough affairs for much of the eighteenth and nineteenth centuries. A few of them were mechanized or planked, but most were simple routes that connected communities. This began to change with the Good Roads movement of the early twentieth century. As of 2021, there are more than seventy-eight thousand miles of paved roads in North Carolina, creating one of the largest highway systems in the United States.

THE KING'S HIGHWAY

In 1660, King Charles II asked the governors in North American to establish a coast road to facilitate communication between the colonies. The 1,300-mile road between Boston and Charleston, known as the King's Highway, was not completed until 1735. The King's Highway skirted west of the Great Dismal Swamp, from Corapeake (Gates County) to Edenton, following modern-day NC 32. After crossing the Chowan River, the route continued south, passing over the Neuse River to New Bern, following US 17. From New Bern, the King's Highway worked its way to Wilmington. There are numerous North Carolina Highway Historical Markers denoting the path of the King's Highway across Eastern North Carolina. These markers are often listed as "First Postal Road" and can be found in Corapeake, Edenton, Bath, New Bern, Belgrade and in Brunswick County on the North Carolina/ South Carolina border.

PLANK ROADS

In the late 1840s, there was a movement to build plank roads in the eastern parts of North Carolina. These wooden roads connected major communities and expedited travel and commerce. The state supported many of these road projects, and by 1860, nearly 500 miles of plank roads had been constructed. The longest stretch was a 129-mile section from Fayetteville to High Point. Other plank roads ran from Cameron to Asheboro and from Warsaw to Greenville and then to Wilson. In the 1850s, the construction of railroads, followed by the outbreak of the Civil War in 1861, led to the demise of such roads. There are North Carolina Highway Historical Markers connected to various plank roads located in Greenville, Wilson, Spout Springs, White Hall, Fayetteville, Bethania, High Point, Cameron, Carthage and Asheboro.

Plank roads, like the one illustrated here, were common connections between major towns in eighteenth- and nineteenth-century North Carolina. *State Archives of North Carolina.*

WARRIOR'S PATH/GREAT PHILADELPHIA WAGON ROAD, FORSYTH COUNTY

Originally called the Warrior's Path, the Great Philadelphia Wagon Road became one of the most important roads in colonial America. It began in Philadelphia, passing through Maryland and the Shenandoah Valley in Virginia before entering North Carolina in present-day Stokes County. The road passed through the communities of Germanton, Winston, Salem, Salisbury and Charlotte before continuing south into South Carolina and Georgia. Thousands of settlers recently arrived in Pennsylvania used the route to reach the interior of the colonies. The route was also used by traders, moving furs to market and returning with supplies for the early settlers. The route was also a major thoroughfare during the American Revolution. There is a North Carolina Highway Historical Marker located in the Historic Bethabara Park in Bethania.

DANIEL BOONE MOTOR TRAIL

Daniel Boone is America's best-known pioneer hero. Born in Pennsylvania in 1734, he lived in North Carolina for twenty-one years before moving west to Kentucky. He lived on the Yadkin River in present-day Davie County. Boone spent months every fall "long hunting" in the mountains of Western North Carolina, and a score of places in the state are named for him or members of his family. Boone's Cave Park in Davidson County is one of those early sites associated with the Boone family. The town of Boone was an early camping site for Boone while hunting. On the grounds of Appalachian State University, there is a monument depicting Boone. Beginning in the early twentieth century, Hamp Rich, a Davie County native, began a project to create the Boone Trail Highway. Rich marked his motor trail with plaques bearing Boone's likeness. These plaques, often including metal from the battleship USS *Maine*, were mounted inside large arrowheads. Rich's project was in competition with another motor trail honoring Boone, this one being organized by the Daughters of the American Revolution. The Boone Trail Highway eventually stretched all over the United States, from Massachusetts to California. Few examples remain from the seventy-two or more markers that were placed in North Carolina. Daniel Boone Highway Memorial Association markers that do survive are located in Winston-Salem, Old Fort, Pembroke, Lumberton,

Wilkesboro has one of the most impressive Daniel Boone Motor Trail markers in the state. *State Archives of North Carolina.*

Chapel Hill, Sanford, Stanley, East Bend, Montreat, Hickory, Sparta, Mocksville, Hillsborough, Statesville, Wilkesboro and North Wilkesboro. There are also several museums with displays on Daniel Boone, including the Rowan County Museum in Salisbury and the Wilkes County Museum in Wilkesboro.

JEFFERSON DAVIS MEMORIAL HIGHWAY

Planned to be a transcontinental highway, the Jefferson Davis Memorial Highway was named in honor of Jefferson Davis, former U.S. senator, secretary of war and Confederate president. The project was begun by the United Daughters of the Confederacy in 1913. The highway began in Arlington, Virginia, and ran south into North Carolina. It followed current US 15 through Durham and Chapel Hill to Sanford, then US 1 from Sanford to the South Carolina line. There were numerous concrete markers along the route, but most have been removed.

BUNCOMBE TURNPIKE

Like the King's Highway and the Great Wagon Road, the Buncombe Turnpike became one of the major north–south thoroughfares in North Carolina. Travel through the mountains was tedious and difficult, with even more challenges than those encountered in other parts of the state. While roads down east might have to contend with river crossings, mountain roads had to cross rivers, travel through mountain passes and make switchbacks. The Buncombe Turnpike was created in 1824 and was constructed between 1827 and 1828. It was seventy-five miles in length and connected Tennessee with South Carolina. From the north, the road passed through Paint Gap in Madison County and then down through Asheville, Hendersonville and Flat Rock before entering South Carolina at Saluda Gap. There is a North Carolina Highway Historical Marker concerning the road in Asheville.

BLUE RIDGE PARKWAY

A road along the crest of the Blue Ridge Mountains had been the dream of many different individuals for several decades. In 1906, Joseph H. Pratt, the state geologist, promoted the "Crest of the Blue Ridge Highway," a toll road running between Marion, Virginia, and Tallulah, Georgia. Construction finally commenced in 1911, and a section between Linville in Avery County and Altapass in Mitchell County was completed by 1913. Another proposed scenic trail in the mountains was the Black Bear Trail, stretching from Quebec, through New York, Pennsylvania and Virginia and then into North Carolina. It was planned to pass through Sparta, Jefferson, Boone and Blowing Rock, past Grandfather Mountain and through Linville, eventually reaching Florida. World War I, followed by the Great Depression, put a stop to many of these projects.

The idea of the Blue Ridge Parkway began in 1933. It was a recreational road connecting the Shenandoah National Park in Virginia with the Great Smoky Mountains National Park on the North Carolina/Tennessee border. The project employed engineers, architects, stonemasons and many local people in a time when jobs were few. Construction began on September 11, 1935, near Cumberland Knob, Alleghany County, North Carolina. Finally, in 1987, the last link, 7.7 miles around the side of Grandfather Mountain, was completed, and the parkway was finished. Overall, it is 469 miles in length and not open to commercial traffic. In North Carolina, the parkway

The Blue Ridge Parkway has numerous interpretive markers, such as this one in Ashe County, describing Mount Jefferson. *Author's collection.*

passes by Grandfather Mountain, the Orchard at Altapass and Mount Mitchell, ending in Cherokee. There is a North Carolina Highway Historical Marker at Cumberland Knob, and the parkway includes several worthwhile museums or historic sites, such as the Moses Cone Memorial Park, Linn Cove Viaduct Visitor Center and the Southern Highlands Folk Art Center.

Further Reading:

Randell Jones, *Trailing Daniel Boone: Daughters of the American Revolution Marking Daniel Boone's Trail, 1912–1915* (2012)

Parke Rouse, *The Great Wagon Road: From Philadelphia to the South* (1992)

Anne Mitchell Whisnant, *Super-Scenic Motorway: A Blue Ridge Parkway History* (2006)

WOVEN THROUGH THE PAST

THE TEXTILE INDUSTRY

North Carolina's textile history is measured in centuries. Early settlers grew flax and raised sheep, set up spinning wheels and looms and produced their own clothes. Europeans discovered cotton in the Bahamas in 1492, and soon its cultivation spread, reaching the Carolina colonies by the 1600s. The first cotton mill in North Carolina, the Schenck-Warlick Mill, was established in Lincoln County in 1814. By 1860, there were 45 textile mills, processing cotton and wool, in North Carolina. During the Civil War, many mills manufactured cloth for Confederate uniforms, blankets, shirts, underwear, sacks and bags. The war wrecked many of the mills, but they rebounded quickly. By 1884, there were 75 mills in the state. By 1900, there were 200, and by 1931, the number had grown to 343. In 2000, there were 386 textile mills, employing 63,300 people in the state. However, competition from foreign markets, especially after the passage of the North American Free Trade Agreement, has diminished the textile industry in North Carolina.

TEXTILE HERITAGE MUSEUM, ALAMANCE COUNTY

Housed in the Glencoe Mills Company Store, the Textile Heritage Museum sits in what is considered the most complete mill village surviving in the United States. The museum tells the story of the industry, from picking the cotton to the manufacture of cloth. Glencoe Mills was established in the 1880s by brothers James H. and William E. Holt. They produced napped

There were, at one time, hundreds of cotton and woolen mills across North Carolina. *State Archives of North Carolina.*

cotton cloth, flannels and woven plaids. In 1954, the mill ceased production. The site was added to the National Register of Historic Places in 1979.

TEXTILE HERITAGE CENTER, DAVIE COUNTY

The Cooleemee Cotton Mill was built in 1899–1900 and, in 1906, was renamed the Erwin Cotton Mill Company. A substantial mill town grew up around the mill, including a section for African American workers. The mill finally closed in 1967. The Cooleemee Historical Association operates two museums. The Zachary House was built in 1923 and is the primary museum, while the Mill House, constructed in 1903, shows visitors the life of a millworker in 1923. Collectively, these are known as the Textile Heritage Center Museum.

COLEMAN MANUFACTURING COMPANY, CABARRUS COUNTY

By the 1890s, Warren C. Coleman had become the wealthiest Black man in North Carolina. His business interests were diverse, and in 1897, he began a textile mill project in Concord. He had both Black and White partners and constructed the Coleman Cotton Mill. The mill hired only Black workers. This was the first Black-owned textile mill in the United States. After Coleman's death in 1904, the mill was acquired by Benjamin Duke and then by Fieldcrest Cannon. A North Carolina Highway Historical Marker is located in Concord.

HAW RIVER HISTORICAL MUSEUM, ALAMANCE COUNTY

The Haw River area, near Burlington, had two textile mills. The Granite Mill opened in 1844, eventually becoming the world's largest manufacturer of corduroy. This mill was later owned by Cannon Mills. The Holt-Tabardrey Mill opened in 1898 and is sometimes referred to as the Granite Cora-Holt Mill. Located on the edge of town, the Haw River Historical Museum contains looms from various eras and information on the different textile mills in the area.

ALAMANCE COTTON MILL, ALAMANCE COUNTY

Constructed by Edwin M. Holt in 1837, the Alamance Cotton Mill produced the first colored fabrics south of the Potomac River. Holt's sons went on to establish the mills in Glencoe. The Holts purchased other mills as well, and

Edwin Holt was one of the leaders in the textile industry in North Carolina. *Courtesy of the State Archives of North Carolina.*

for almost ninety years, the family dominated the textile industry in North Carolina. There is a North Carolina Highway Historical Marker concerning the Alamance Cotton Mill in Alamance.

ROCKY MOUNT MILLS, NASH COUNTY

The second textile mill built in North Carolina, Rocky Mount Mills, opened in 1818 on the falls of the Tar River. The mill was run by enslaved people until women and children became the labor force in 1852. In July 1863, the mill was burned by Federal soldiers. After it was rebuilt, the textile mill continued to be a leader in the state until it was forced to close in 1996. There is a North Carolina Highway Historical Marker in Rocky Mount.

MOUNT HECLA MILL, GUILFORD COUNTY

Completed in 1834, the Mount Hecla Mill was the first steam-powered mill in North Carolina and possibly the first in the South. Previously, mills were only constructed near significant water sources. The Mount Hecla Mill was built by Henry Humphreys and was the third textile mill built in the state. Humphreys also built Blandwood, later the home of Governor John Motley Morehead. There is a North Carolina Highway Historical Marker marking the location of the Mount Hecla Mill in Greensboro.

PROXIMITY MILL, GUILFORD COUNTY

A second wave of textile mill construction developed in the decades after the Civil War. Brothers Moses and Ceasar Cone started out in the wholesale business in New York City in 1891. In 1893, they moved to Greensboro. Two years later, they opened their own mill, naming it the Proximity Mill. In 1899, they opened Revolution Mill, which became the world's largest flannel mill. Then came the White Oak Mill in the early 1900s, the largest cotton mill in the South and eventually the largest denim manufacturer in the world. Moses Cone eventually became known as the "Denim King." He owned the Cone Manor House, now a part of the Blue Ridge Parkway. A North Carolina Highway Historical Marker is in Greensboro near the site of the original mill.

LORAY MILL, GASTON COUNTY

Employing 3,500 workers, the Loray Mill in Gastonia was the largest single mill employer in the state in 1928. It was also owned by outside interests, who cut the workforce to 2,200 and reduced wages for the remaining employees. Outside labor unions, including the communist National Textile Workers Union, arrived in 1929 and, on April 1, 1929, induced the workers to strike. The workers requested a forty-hour workweek, minimum pay of twenty dollars per week and union recognition. In response, employees' families were evicted from mill-owned homes, and the local mayor asked Governor O. Max Gardner for help. The governor sent in National Guard soldiers. There were several confrontations over the next few weeks, including one in which Police Chief Aderholt was killed. Eventually, seventy-one strikers and eight members of the NTWU were arrested. Sixteen people were indicted for the murder of the police chief, but the trial ended in a mistrial. Following this, a truck carrying twenty-two strikers was chased down and fired on, with one female striker being killed. When the Aderholt case was retried, six millworkers were found guilty of second-degree murder and sentenced to prison terms. The woman killed, Ella May Wiggins, was a union organizer and balladeer; partially due to her death, mill owners adjusted hours and provided better working conditions. There is a North Carolina Highway Historical Marker in Gastonia.

Further Reading:
Brent D. Glass, *The Textile Industry in North Carolina: A History* (1992)

"MADE IN NORTH CAROLINA"

TAR HEEL FOOD AND BEVERAGE CREATIONS

North Carolina is well known for several distinct foodstuffs, like barbecue (both eastern and western styles), along with another regional favorite, livermush. While each of these might be an acquired taste, there are several North Carolina–created eatables that are popular across the South and the United States.

PEPSI, CRAVEN COUNTY

In 1893, New Bern pharmacist Caleb Bradham created "Brad's Drink." It was made of water, sugar, caramel, lemon oil, nutmeg and kola nuts. Given the popularity of "Brad's Drink," he changed the name to Pepsi-Cola and started selling it at his pharmacy. The name was trademarked in 1903, and the syrup was sold to other vendors across North Carolina. Bottling companies were established in Charlotte and Durham. By 1910, there were 240 franchises across twenty-four states. The company passed out of Bradham's hands in 1923. Corporate offices are now in New York. There are several places in New Bern to check out the history of Pepsi, including the Pepsi Store. New Bern has a North Carolina Highway Historical Marker dedicated to Bradham.

Pepsi started in North Carolina as Brad's Drink. *State Archives of North Carolina.*

MT. OLIVE PICKLES/MOUNT OLIVE MUSEUM, WAYNE COUNTY

The Mt. Olive Pickle Company started out as a wholesale cucumber company, selling to other picklers. When business did not thrive, the owners began pickling their own cucumbers, and in 1926, the company flourished. The entrepreneur was Lebanese immigrant Shikrey Baddour, who was joined by other local businesspeople. Today, Mt. Olive Pickle Company is the largest privately held pickle company in the Unites States. A tour is offered at the Mt. Olive Pickle Company. The Mount Olive Museum has an exhibit on the pickle company.

KRISPY KREME, FORSYTH COUNTY

Vernon Rudolph's family was invested in the doughnut-making business. They had purchased a doughnut recipe from a French chef and tried to establish the business in Paducah, Kentucky, and Nashville, Tennessee. However, the ongoing Great Depression impeded their success, so Vernon moved to Winston-Salem in 1937 and opened a shop across from Salem College, a site now commemorated with a historical marker. At first, he sold to local grocery stores, but upon request, he began selling to customers on the street. Rudolph developed a machine that allowed each store to make hot, fresh doughnuts on site. The company was sold to Beatrice Foods Company after the death of Rudolph in the 1970s, but it was purchased by a group of Krispy Kreme franchisees in 1982. Corporate headquarters are still located in Winston-Salem, and customers can watch doughnuts being made at any of the thirty-one shops in North Carolina, as well as at the many other locations across the country.

CHEERWINE, ROWAN COUNTY

Sodas were all the rage in the early twentieth century. Small companies sprang up seemingly overnight. During a sugar shortage in 1917, L.D. Peeler purchased a cherry flavor from a St. Louis salesman, added some other flavors and created the widely popular drink Cheerwine at his home in Salisbury. Cheerwine is the country's oldest family-owned soft drink company that is still in business today. There is an annual Cheerwine Festival in Salisbury every May. The Rowan Museum in Salisbury has a Cheerwine exhibit that features early bottles and examples of advertising.

BOJANGLES, MECKLENBURG COUNTY

Bojangles was founded by Richard Thomas and Jack Fulk in Charlotte in 1977. The restaurant was named after the 1968 song "Mr. Bojangles" by Jerry Jeff Walker. There are now more than seven hundred Bojangles restaurants, with the majority in North Carolina.

TEXAS PETE, FORSYTH COUNTY

Sam Garner owned and operated the Dixie Pig barbecue stand in Winston-Salem in the 1920s. The Garner family had already developed a barbecue sauce. When his customers asked for a spicier sauce, he developed one with cayenne peppers, and the family named it "Texas Pete." In 1946, the family founded the T.W. Garner Food Company, making jams, jellies, horseradish, hot dog chili, seafood cocktail sauce and a Buffalo wing sauce, among others. Texas Pete is still one of the top-selling hot sauces in the United States.

LANCE CRACKERS, MECKLENBURG COUNTY

Philip Lance had five hundred pounds of unwanted peanuts. It was 1913, and he needed something to do with the legumes. So he roasted them and sold them for a nickel a bag. He soon went into business with his son-in-law, Salem Van Every, and founded the Lance Packing Company in Charlotte. They invested in a mechanical roaster and manufactured peanut butter that was spread on crackers, creating the first commercially sold peanut butter cracker in the United States. Soldiers at nearby Camp Greene could not get enough of them. In 1938, Lance began making its own crackers. The company continued after the deaths of both the owners. In 1954, Lance started using vending machines and, in the 1980s, began selling to grocery stores. The cracker company is still headquartered in Charlotte.

HWY 55 BURGERS, SHAKES & FRIES, WAYNE COUNTY

While not an old company, Hwy 55 Burgers is one of North Carolina's most popular. Founded by Kenney Moore, the first burger shop opened in a mall in Goldsboro in 1991 under the name of Andy's. By 2005, there were one hundred Andy's locations in North Carolina. Soon thereafter, the name was changed to Hwy 55 Burgers, Shakes & Fries. The headquarters are now located in Mount Olive.

HARDEE'S, PITT COUNTY

Wilber Hardee opened his first restaurant in Greenville in September 1960. Hoping to expand, he took on partners, and a second store was opened in

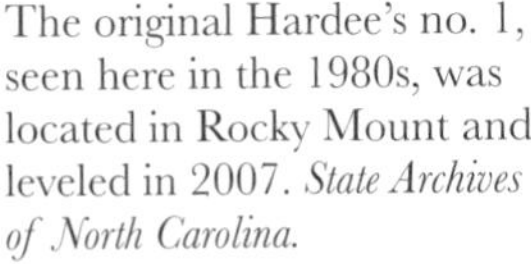
The original Hardee's no. 1, seen here in the 1980s, was located in Rocky Mount and leveled in 2007. *State Archives of North Carolina.*

Rocky Mount in 1961. Wilber Hardee sold his restaurant to his partners, who established a franchise. As of February 2016, there were 5,812 Hardee's restaurants in the United States.

Further Reading:
Bob Garner, *Foods that Make You Say Mmm-mmm* (2014)
John Reed, Dale Reed and William McKinney, *Holy Smoke: The Big Book of North Carolina Barbecue* (2016)

"FIRST IN FLIGHT"

Aviation history goes back more than a century in North Carolina. In 1873, Henry Gatling designed a hand-cranked monoplane in Hertford County. In Mecklenburg County in 1881, Daniel Asbury built a steam-powered monoplane. In 1903, Orville and Wilbur Wright, brothers from Ohio, became the first to make a controlled, powered aircraft flight in the United States. Because of favorable winds, they chose to use Kitty Hawk on the Outer Banks to make that flight. A few years later, Luther Davis of Carteret County built a twin-rotor helicopter. While unmanned and tethered to the ground, it flew between four and five feet off the ground in 1907, making North Carolina the site of the world's first vertical flight. For many reasons, North Carolina truly is "First in Flight."

COASTAL

Wright Brothers National Memorial, Dare County

Two brothers from Ohio, Orville and Wilbur Wright, arrived in the Outer Banks of North Carolina in December 1903. When not working on bicycles in Dayton, they had been building and experimenting with gliders. Now, they had strapped an engine to one of them. They chose the sand dunes of the Outer Banks because of the air currents. The area was desolate, about four miles south of Kitty Hawk. On December 17, they made four flights,

The Wright brothers used the dunes near Kill Devil Hills to make their first flight in 1903. *State Archives of North Carolina.*

the longest lasting twelve seconds. North Carolina became the "First in Flight" state, and the world changed. In March 1927, Congress authorized the establishment of the Kill Devil Hill(s) Monument. In 1953, the name changed to the Wright Brothers National Memorial. The site tells the story of the Wright brothers' historic flight. There is a visitors' center with a replica Wright Flyer, a replica hangar, monuments, markers and the field itself. A North Carolina Highway Historical Marker is nearby.

PIEDMONT

Tiny Broadwick, Vance County

At just over four feet tall, Tiny Broadwick was just that. But she was fearless. In 1913, she became the first woman to parachute from an airplane. Broadwick, born Georgia Ann Thompson in 1893 on a farm in Granville

Parachutist Tiny Broadwick sits in position on the jump seat, with Glenn L. Martin preparing to pilot the plane. *State Archives of North Carolina.*

County, saw a man parachute out of a balloon at the state fair in Raleigh in 1907. She joined the troupe, parachuting out of a balloon in 1908. With the advent of airplanes, she switched from balloons to the new invention, parachuting all over the United States. Due to health reasons, she made her last jump in 1922. There is a North Carolina Highway Historical Marker near the site of her grave in Vance County.

Maynard Field, Forsyth County

Lieutenant Belvin Maynard, known as the "Flying Parson," was a Sampson County native and one of the world's foremost aviators. A graduate of Wake Forest College, after his ordination, Maynard enlisted in the U.S. Army Air Corps, becoming a test pilot for the American Expeditionary Force in France. Following the war, he returned to Wake Forest to pursue more education but also kept flying. Maynard became the first person to conduct a marriage

Lieutenant Belvin Maynard, the Flying Parson, is pictured with others in Raleigh in 1920. *State Archives of North Carolina.*

ceremony while airborne, established a world record of 313 loop-the-loops, won the first transcontinental air derby and became the first to fly from New York to Chicago between a sunrise and a sunset. He was one of the world's foremost pilots. In 1919, in an effort to win the contract for a stopover for the U.S. Mail, the board of trade in Winston-Salem leased property and established an airfield. Maynard was the first person to land at the new facility, which was then nothing more than a field, so the airport was named in his honor. It became the site of the first commercial airfield in North Carolina. Maynard was killed in a crash in September 1922 in Vermont and buried at the family cemetery in Sampson County. Maynard Field continued to operate until the mid-1930s. A historic marker was erected in Winston-Salem in 2008.

Lindley Field, Guilford County

Most early airfields in North Carolina were simply farmers' fields. A newspaper would advertise an airshow, and people from far and wide would gather to watch planes come in, land and then take off again, performing aerobatics for those on the ground. Often, celebrities were a part of these shows and dedications. When the Raleigh Municipal Airport was dedicated in 1929, Eddie Rickenbacker, the World War I flying ace, was on hand, as was Charles Lindbergh in the *Spirit of St. Louis*. Amelia Earhart arrived in 1931 to christen a new airplane. Alas, nothing of that field remains today. Greensboro's Lindley Field opened in 1927, with passenger service beginning in July that year. On May 1, 1928, an airplane landed with airmail, a first for North Carolina. Problems closed the airport in 1935, but it reopened in 1937 with two new paved runways and a passenger terminal. During World War II, the airport was used by the U.S. Army Air Corps and was a hub for the Overseas Replacement Depot. The airport continued to expand and is known today as the Piedmont Triad International Airport. A North Carolina Highway Historical Marker is in Greensboro.

North Carolina Aviation Museum and Hall of Fame, Randolph County

Founded in 1994 as the Foundation for Aircraft Conservation, the North Carolina Aviation Museum has an impressive collection of aircraft, including a World War II B-25 "Mitchell" bomber, a Piper J-3 Flitfire flown by Orville Wright, several other aircraft, engines and even a 1948 Lincoln limousine that belonged to President Harry Truman. The museum also houses the North Carolina Aviation Hall of Fame.

Carolinas Aviation Museum, Mecklenburg County

Located beside the Charlotte Douglas International Airport and founded in 1992, the Carolinas Aviation Museum has a diverse collection of aircraft and aviation memorabilia, including the "Miracle on the Hudson," a passenger jet that landed in New York's Hudson River in 2009. Other airplanes include a DC-7B, a DC-3, a Sopwith Camel, an AV-8B Harrier II and a P-80 Shooting Star. Starting in 2019, the Carolinas Aviation Museum underwent a revamping, with plans to reopen in 2023 with a new STEM focus.

Hickory Aviation Museum, Catawba County

While some aviation museums in North Carolina have a broad focus, the Hickory Aviation Museum focuses specifically on the "Golden Age of Aviation." All of the pieces in its collection are military aircraft. Much of the museum is devoted to military personnel from the Greater Hickory area, and the exhibits include uniforms, photographs, models and stories. Outside on the tarmac are more than a dozen planes and helicopters, including the only surviving Curtiss XF15C-1 "Stingeree," a prototype U.S. Navy carrier-based fighter. There is also a Beechcraft T-34 "Mentor," a Grumman F-14D "Tomcat," a Lockheed P-3C Orion that is open for tours and a World War II vintage Fm-2 "Wildcat."

North Carolina Transportation Museum, Rowan County

While much of the North Carolina Transportation Museum focuses on the railroad history of North Carolina, the museum also has a sizable display on North Carolina's aviation history. This includes information on Piedmont Airlines, a commercial carrier founded in North Carolina in 1948, with headquarters in Winston-Salem. In the 1980s, Piedmont Airlines had a fleet of 177 aircraft carrying more than 20 million passengers to 235 locations. U.S. Air purchased Piedmont Airlines in the late 1980s. The museum has a Piedmont airplane undergoing restoration. The museum also features a replica of the Wright Flyer.

Piedmont Airlines was a commercial carrier founded in North Carolina in 1948. *State Archives of North Carolina.*

MOUNTAINS

The Western North Carolina Air Museum, Henderson County

The oldest aviation museum in North Carolina was founded in 1989 with the goal of preserving the aviation history of Western North Carolina. It has several different types of aircraft and has hosted several special visitors, including President George W. Bush, who visited in 1992. Several of the planes here are almost one hundred years old, including a 1927 Waco 10, and there are also several replica planes, including a 1915 Morane Saulnier, a 1917 Se-5A and a 1917 Curtiss Jenny JN-4D. The hangar is full of models and posters of other aircraft.

Further Reading:

David McCullough, *The Wright Brothers* (2015)

Thomas C. Parramore, *First to Fly: North Carolina and the Beginnings of Aviation* (2002)

REACHING FOR THE STARS FROM THE TAR HEEL STATE

THE SPACE RACE

When people think of U.S. locations important to the Space Race, North Carolina does not often come to the top of the list. Sites in Florida, Maryland, Texas and California are usually at the forefront of that history. Yet North Carolina, like most other states, played an important role and made unique contributions as the United States reached for the stars.

Some of the state's biggest contributions were people. James E. Webb was born in Tally Ho, Granville County, on October 7, 1906. After graduating from University of North Carolina–Chapel Hill in 1928, Webb went on to serve in the U.S. Marine Corps as an aviator and obtained a law degree. He served on numerous political staffs over the years, including those of U.S. Representative Edward W. Pou and Undersecretary of the Treasury Oliver Max Gardner, and then served as President Harry Truman's undersecretary of state. In February 1961, Webb was appointed administrator of NASA by President John F. Kennedy. Webb was largely responsible for overseeing the Apollo program. In 1969, Webb received the Presidential Medal of Freedom and, in 1976, the Langley Gold Medal from the Smithsonian Institution. He died in 1992 and is buried at Arlington National Cemetery.

Although Christopher Kraft was born in Virginia, his mother was born in Lenoir. In a 1967 *Charlotte Observer* article, Kraft described spending much of his childhood in Lenoir and Linville Falls. After finishing a degree at Virginia Tech, Kraft went on to become an engineer with NASA, working on the Mercury program. In 1958, he became the very first flight director.

He was on duty during the first American crewed spaceflight, first crewed orbital flight and first spacewalk.

Christine (Mann) Darden was one of the Black women hired at Langley Research Center in 1967 to work as a human computer. Darden was the first woman to be promoted into the Senior Executive Service at Langley and is featured in the book *Hidden Figures*. She was awarded the Congressional Gold Medal in 2019. Born in Monroe in 1942, she attended local schools, including Allen High School in Asheville. Darden was considered "one of NASA's preeminent experts on supersonic flight and sonic booms."

Sam Beddington was born in Clayton in 1933. After graduating from North Carolina State, he worked for the U.S. Air Force and then NASA starting in 1959. Beddington was one of the few who worked on the Mercury, Gemini, Apollo and Space Shuttle programs. He retired in 1985 as deputy director of shuttle operations and passed away in 2010.

Myrtle "Kay" Cagle should have become a household name. Born in 1925 in Selma, she learned to fly from her brothers at the age of twelve and became the youngest pilot in North Carolina at the age of fourteen. She joined the Civil Air Patrol and the Ninety-Nines but was not tall enough to join the WASP. Following World War II, she wrote aviation columns for newspapers in Selma and Raleigh and went on to operate a flight school. Cagle married, moved to Georgia and participated in the Women in Space Program, eventually becoming a part of the Mercury 13, a group of women scheduled to be the first female astronauts. After that program was canceled, she taught at Robins Air Force Base and continued to fly. Prior to her death in 2019, she was inducted into the Georgia Aviation Hall of Fame and awarded an honorary doctorate from the University of Wisconsin–Oshkosh.

Several astronauts were born in North Carolina: Charlie Duke, Apollo 16 (Charlotte); William E. Thorton, STS-8 and STS-51-B (Faison); Ellen S. Baker, STS-34, STS-50 and STS-71 (Fayetteville); Curtis Brown, STS-47, STS-66, STS-77, STS-85, STS-96 and STS-103 (Elizabethtown); Michael J. Smith, STS-51 (Beaufort); Susan J. Helms, STS-54, STS-64, STS-78, STS-101 and STS-102/105 (Charlotte); William S. McArthur, STS-58; STS-74, STS-92 and Soyuz TMA-7 (Laurinburg); Charles E. Brady Jr., STS-78 (Pinehurst); and Thomas Mashburn, STS-127 and Soyuz TMA-07M (Statesville).

COASTAL

In Beaufort, a North Carolina Highway Historical Marker to astronaut Michael J. Smith, who died in the 1986 *Challenger* disaster, was dedicated in 2018.

In Oxford, a North Carolina Highway Historical Marker for James Webb, marking his childhood home, was dedicated in 2018.

In Wakulla, there is a local highway historical marker for William S. McArthur.

PIEDMONT

Morehead Planetarium, Orange County

Constructed in 1949, the Morehead Planetarium was the first planetarium in the South and the first located on a university campus. At the time of its construction, it was the most expensive building in North Carolina. The projector came from Germany. From 1959 until 1975, every astronaut, except Harrison Schmitt, was trained in celestial navigation at the planetarium. Several astronauts had to use their training on actual flights, including Gordon Cooper on the Mercury *Faith 7* flight and the members of Apollo 12, after lightning strikes knocked their systems offline. The planetarium is

Morehead Planetarium was used to train early astronauts in celestial navigation. *Author's collection.*

open to the public and has several exhibits on early telescopes and on the Mercury, Gemini and Apollo astronauts. Also located on site is the Morehead Observatory, which houses a twenty-four-inch telescope open to the public on Friday evenings. Morehead Planetarium is located on the campus of the University of North Carolina–Chapel Hill.

Burlington Mill, Caldwell/Burke Counties

Once the world's largest textile company, Burlington Industries in Rhodhiss manufactured fabrics used in space shields, protecting craft as they reentered the atmosphere, and wove the material used by Apollo astronauts and the flags left behind on the moon.

MOUNTAINS

Rosman Tracking Station, Transylvania County

To communicate with the Apollo spacecraft, NASA constructed several tracking stations, including one southwest of Asheville near Rosman. The station was known as the Rosman Satellite Tracking and Data Acquisition Facility. The facility was dedicated in October 1963, boasting two twenty-six-meter radio telescopes, plus the necessary support buildings. At its peak, the site employed 350 people. In 1981, the site was transferred to the

The Rosman Tracking Facility, built by NASA, was used during the Apollo program. *Author's collection.*

Department of Defense, and in 1995, it was closed. In 1999, the site was purchased by a private party who transferred it to the Pisgah Astronomical Research Institute (PARI). The radio telescopes were returned to operation. Today, the site is primarily used to encourage students to reach for the stars.

A-B Emblem, Buncombe County

One of the most iconic pieces of a space mission is the patch worn by the astronauts. In 1962, A-B Emblem in Weaverville designed the original NASA logo, "the Meat Ball." There were no mission patches until 1965, when Gordon Cooper and Pete Conrad designed their own patch for the Gemini 5 mission. NASA embraced the idea; now all teams design a patch for their missions. Since 1970, the patches have been manufactured by A-B Emblems in Weaverville. The patches for Virgin Galactic and SpaceX are also manufactured at this facility.

Further Reading:
W. Henry Lambright, *Powering Apollo: James W. Webb of NASA* (1995)
Margot Lee Shetterly, *Hidden Figures: The American Dream and the Untold Story of the Black Women Who Helped Win the Space Race* (2016)
Amy Shira Teitel, *Fighting for Space* (2021)

ECLECTIC MUSEUMS AND HISTORIC SITES

There are some stories, often connected with historic sites and museums, that just don't fit into neat categories. North Carolina has its fair share of these unique sites and markers that help tell about easily overlooked pieces of the past.

COASTAL

New Bern Firemen's Museum, Craven County

The New Bern Firemen's Museum, established in 1955, tells the story of two different fire companies: the Atlantic Hook & Ladder Company and the New Bern Steam Fire Engine Company No. 1. Housed in an actual fire department, the museum walks visitors through a century and a half of firefighting history, from the days of hand-pumped engines through the fire trucks of the twentieth century. The museum also features an exhibit on the great fire of 1922 that wiped out one thousand buildings, the most destructive fire in North Carolina history.

Millie and Christine McKoy, Columbus County

Called the "Carolina Twins" or the "Two-Headed Nightingale," Millie and Christine McKoy (1851–1912) were African American conjoined twins.

Millie and Christine McKoy were African American conjoined twins born in North Carolina. *State Archives of North Carolina.*

They were born enslaved in Whiteville, sold before they were one year old and put on exhibition. They were showcased across the United States prior to gaining their freedom when the Thirteenth Amendment was ratified in December 1865. Their former owner, Joseph P. Smith, provided them an education. They could sing, dance, play music and speak five languages. They even met Queen Victoria. They continued to perform for a number of years, eventually returning to North Carolina. There is a North Carolina Highway Historical Marker near at their birthplace near Whiteville.

St. Thomas Church, Beaufort County

Among the many historic structures in the town of Bath is St. Thomas Episcopal Church. The brick building was constructed in 1734 and is the oldest church building in North Carolina. St. Thomas Parish was established in 1696, and with books mailed from England around 1700, it became the first library in the colony. There is a North Carolina Highway Historical Marker in Bath.

PIEDMONT

Battle of Alamance, Alamance County

There has been more than one "rebellion" in North Carolina. In 1771, some local residents in the northern Piedmont area, the Regulators, became upset over the issues of taxation and corrupt local officials. Governor William Tryon called out the militia and marched to the Hillsborough area. The Regulators asked to meet with Tryon to work out their differences, but Tryon stated that he would only do so after they had laid down their arms. The Battle of Alamance soon resulted, and after two hours of fighting, the militia carried the day. Six of the Regulators were later hanged in Hillsborough. The location of the battle is now the Alamance Battlefield State Park, with a visitors' center, the 1780 John Allen House, monuments and hiking trails. There is also a North Carolina Highway Historical Marker nearby.

Eng and Chang Bunker, Surry County

Born in present-day Thailand, Chang and Eng Bunker (1811–1874) were conjoined twins who came to the United States in 1829. They spent a decade touring before retiring to a farm near Mount Airy, where they became American citizens, married sisters and bought slaves. They then toured occasionally. Every three days, they journeyed to the other brother's home; they eventually fathered twenty-one children and died within hours of each other. The Mount Airy Regional Museum has a display on their lives, and there is a North Carolina Highway Historical Marker near their graves in White Plains.

County Doctor Museum, Nash County

While the twentieth century gave rise to hospitals, local doctors remained prevalent in many rural communities. The Country Doctor Museum in

Bailey has an impressive display on doctors, as well as exhibits on nurses and an apothecary. Created in 1967, the museum contains more than five thousand artifacts and is managed by East Carolina University's Laupus Health Sciences Library. There is a North Carolina Highway Historical Marker nearby.

Museum of Early Southern Decorative Arts, Forsyth County

Old Salem is an absolute treasure in North Carolina history. Beyond the collection of original houses and shops is the Museum of Early Southern Decorative Arts, which opened in 1965. The museum is considered the foremost research center when it comes to southern decorative arts and material culture. Included in the collection are paintings, firearms, pottery and more. There is also a library that focuses heavily on North Carolina and southern craftspeople and furniture.

Tobacco Farm Life Museum, Johnston County

The importance of tobacco in North Carolina history cannot be overstated. Following the Civil War years, tobacco was the primary crop in the state, employing thousands of people who grew, processed and transported tobacco. Founded in 1983, the Tobacco Farm Life Museum in Kenley preserves and explores the life of the tobacco farmer. On the grounds are a farmhouse, kitchen, smokehouse and a log tobacco barn, a sight once common across the state.

Fort Dobbs State Historic Site, Iredell County

When the French and Indian War comes up for discussion, North Carolina is often overlooked, but the colony did have a role to play in the early conflict. About half of the soldiers from North Carolina went to fight in Virginia and New York. The others stayed to protect the frontier against the Cherokees. Named for Royal Governor Arthur Dobbs, Fort Dobbs was the only permanent period fort constructed in the interior of North Carolina. In February 1760, the garrison at Fort Dobbs came under attack by the Cherokees, who were easily repulsed. The French and Indian War came to an end in 1761 in North America, and the garrison was soon dismissed. Archaeological excavations began in the 1960s, and the actual location of the fort was found in 1968. A reconstruction of Fort Dobbs was completed in September 2019. There is a North Carolina Highway Historical Marker near the reconstructed fort. The site offers tours and living history demonstrations.

Governor Charles B. Aycock Birthplace State Historic Site, Wayne County

Known as the "Education Governor," Charles Aycock (1859–1912) was born in Wayne County and graduated from the University of North Carolina–Chapel Hill. In Goldsboro, Aycock began practicing law, and from 1893 to 1897, he was the U.S. attorney for the Eastern District of North Carolina. Aycock played a large role in the Democratic Party's "white supremacy" campaign that led to the 1898 Wilmington insurrection. Aycock became governor in 1900 and sought education reform. Almost seven hundred new school buildings were constructed for both White and Black children while he was in office. The Governor Charles B. Aycock Birthplace State Historic Site opened in 1958 and contains not only the farm where he grew up but also a one-room schoolhouse. At one time, Aycock was one of the most honored governors, largely due to his advocacy for education. There are buildings on college campuses named for him, schools and a statue of him in the U.S. Capitol. His attitudes toward race prior to his governorship have caused many of those honors to be revoked. There is still a North Carolina Highway Historical Marker for his birthplace near Fremont and another near his office in Goldsboro. There is also a monument to Aycock on the grounds of the North Carolina Capitol in Raleigh.

Governor Charles Aycock's home is preserved as a state historic site in Wayne County. *State Archives of North Carolina.*

MOUNTAINS

Gertrude D. McKee, Jackson County

Gertrude McKee (1885–1948), born in Dillsboro, had a strong desire to serve her community. During World War I, she led programs like Liberty Loans, the Salvation Army and War Savings Stamps. She was appointed by the governor to the North Carolina Educational Commission. In 1930, she was elected to the North Carolina Senate, serving three terms. She was the first woman to serve in the state senate. There is a North Carolina Highway Historical Marker near her home in Sylva.

Lillian Exum Clement, Buncombe County

Born near Black Mountain, Lillian Clement (1920–1925) attended local schools and then the Asheville Business College. While working for the Buncombe County Sheriff's Office, she studied law part time, and in 1917, she became the first woman to open her own law practice, focusing on criminal law. Although she could not vote, she beat two male competitors to win a seat in the North Carolina House in 1921, the first woman to serve in the General Assembly. Clement chose not to run for a second term and served as director of the state hospital in Morganton. She died of pneumonia in 1925. There is a North Carolina Highway Historical Marker near her law office in Asheville.

Waldenses Heritage Museum, Burke County

Founded in the twelfth century in the Alps, the Christian Waldenses arrived in the United States in the late nineteenth century. The largest group settled in the foothills and founded the town of Valdese, which was incorporated in 1920. The Waldenses Heritage Museum opened in 1974, telling the history of the Waldenses and showcasing their distinct architectural style. In Valdese there is also a North Carolina Highway Historical Marker concerning the group.

Further Reading:

Marjoleine Kars, *Breaking Loose Together: The Regulator Rebellion in Pre-Revolutionary North Carolina* (2002)

John R. Maass, *The French and Indian War in North Carolina: The Spreading Flames of War* (2013)

INDEX

D

E

F

G

H

I

J

K

L

M

N

O

P

R

S

T

V

W

Y

ABOUT THE AUTHOR

Michael C. Hardy is a widely published author of North Carolina history. He has written about a wide variety of subjects—like Charlotte, Grandfather Mountain and Confederate regiments—in books, articles and blog posts. His ancestors called Surry and Wilkes Counties home during the American Revolution, and he has called the Toe River Valley area home since 1995. In 2010, Hardy was named North Carolina Historian of the Year by the North Carolina Society of Historians. He was also awarded the James I. Robertson Literary Prize by the Robert E. Lee Civil War Library and Research Center in 2018; Volunteer of the Year for the Pisgah District, Blue Ridge Parkway, in 2015; and the Alice Parker Award for Outstanding Work in Literature and Arts from his alma mater, the University of Alabama. His other History Press titles include *Remembering Avery County* (2007); *North Carolina in the Civil War* (2011); *Civil War Charlotte: The Last Capital of the Confederacy* (2012); *Watauga County, North Carolina, in the Civil War* (2013); *The Capitals of the Confederacy: A History* (2015); *Kirk's Civil War Raids Along the Blue Ridge* (2018); and *Lee's Body Guards: The 39th Virginia Cavalry* (2019). When not researching, writing and traveling, he volunteers at historic sites, sharing his love for history.